# Then Sings My Soul

*TOMMY KING*

# *Then* Sings *My Soul*

The Impact of
## Donald and Frances Winters
*on Church Music in the*
*Southern Baptist Convention*

gatekeeper press™
Columbus, Ohio

Then Sings My Soul: The Impact of Donald and Frances Winters on Church Music in the Southern Baptist Convention

Published by Gatekeeper Press
2167 Stringtown Rd, Suite 109
Columbus, OH 43123-2989
www.GatekeeperPress.com

ISBN (hardcover): 9781662913785

ISBN (paperback): 9781662913792

# PREFACE

This wonderful biography is a **celebration** of the accomplishments of Donald and Frances Winters, especially during their years at William Carey College. My late husband, Don Odom, and I shared many fond memories of Dr. Winters as dean, professor, and conductor. Don also had the privilege of having Mrs. Winters as his vocal pedagogy professor the last time she taught the class. It is a great joy to have these memories in the pages of this book. The exceptional effort of Dr. Tommy King to preserve their legacy is greatly appreciated.

Sarah Odom, B.M. '79, M.M. '86

From the very first moment of an impromptu music audition during the summer of 1975, Dr. Donald Winters began investing in my life. I was not one of those much sought-after School of Music recruiting prizes. My limited ability did not matter to him. I soon came to realize that this tireless servant leader was completely focused on mentoring and encouraging all students. He set in motion for me a wonderful educational experience at William Carey. Donald and Frances Winters were models of the highest integrity. To this day my heart overflows with gratitude for the many ways they spoke into my life as a younger follower of Christ Jesus.

Dr. Slater Murphy, B.M. '79

As a pianist from the age of four, it was a challenge to find an appropriate course of musical instruction when, as a sophomore in high school, my own piano teacher revealed she had carried me as far as she could. Dr. Winters at William Carey College (at the time) opened the door for me to begin a degree program that I would eventually complete in the Class of 1980. As my teacher, conductor, mentor and advisor, Dr. Winters instilled in me a sense of respect and accountability for the development of my talent through my education, combined with ample performance opportunities. At the heart of it all was a deep abiding awareness of God's hand in all aspects in preparation for my professional career. I remain humbled and respectful for the wisdom and grace Dr. Winters offered me in the construction of my musical and spiritual foundation, and I thank God for the rich musical heritage of which I am a part because of the opportunities given me at William Carey.

Dr. Phillip Fortenberry, '80


I came to Carey in 1965 with an inadequate background in music, my experience being mostly singing in my rural church choir and in the concert choir at my school, with some piano training thrown in. Being chosen for the Chorale my first year was a tremendous surprise, and it confirmed to me that Carey was where God intended me to be. Dr. and Mrs. Winters taught me many things both in the classroom and outside the classroom. In class, we learned hymnology, vocal pedagogy, music literature, and the mechanics of leading worship. Outside, I learned how to host a gathering of students and how to conduct myself on a choir tour. I am very grateful for the privilege of knowing and being taught by Donald and Frances Winters.

Elizabeth Ferrell Moore, '69

I am so thankful for the impact Dr. and Mrs. Winters had on me during my college experience. I credit Dr. Winters with giving me the courage and the encouragement to become a music major, which was definitely the right course for me to take. Being in the Chorale under his leadership was an experience I will always take pride in because of his constant striving for excellence, and though I never had Mrs. Winters in the classroom, I also respected her extensive knowledge, and the kind, encouraging, and loving spirit she exuded to all of us. They both loved their students and shared their lives, and even their home, with us often. They both have left an indelible mark on my life for which I am always thankful.

Beverly Thames, '70

Donald and Frances Winters, my mentors, bequeathed to me, through the legacy of their lives and teaching, unexcelled examples of professionalism, integrity, and genuine compassion. While absolutely insisting on excellence, they also demonstrated a willingness and ability to know and be known at a deeply personal level. A statement that I recall Mrs. Winters once making may well have characterized their approach to ministry and also served as a guide throughout my career: "Remember, our primary ministry is the presentation of a person rather than a program."

Bennett Britt, '64

# FOREWORD

Preserving the legacy of Donald and Frances Winters has been a burning desire of mine for many years. This couple had a profound impact on my life, as well as the lives of hundreds of students who studied under them. I had hoped that someone else would take on the responsibility, but as time passed and so many of the Winterses' contemporaries have passed from the scene, it became apparent to me that their legacy will be lost if someone does not take up the task of preserving it. With that in mind, I began the project in the fall of 2020. So much material is available that it became a matter of collecting and summarizing it. I wish to acknowledge that the core of this volume is taken from files and narratives compiled by Frances Winters during her lifetime. Additional material has been found in the *Atlanta Constitution, the Louisville Courier-Journal,* church newsletters from First Baptist Church, Atlanta, the Archives of the Southern Baptist Theological Seminary, the I.E. Rouse Library of William Carey University, and numerous interviews with former students and colleagues. If everything were included, it would take several books. My goal is to produce a volume that can be easily kept in a personal or school library and retrieved at will as a reference source.

Many people are due an expression of gratitude, beginning with Dr. Donald Eugene Winters, the Winterses' son. Members of the chorale during Dr. Winters' tenure provided much information, and students of Frances enhanced the appreciation for the team effort of the couple. Thanks to all who contributed to this effort.

Tommy King

# EARLY LIFE

From the beginning of settlements in the South, music has been a significant part of worship. Farmhands sang while "chopping" or picking cotton or performing other labor as a way of relieving the drudgery of their hard work. Without the luxury of musical instruments, Southern white churches relied on sacred harp music to enliven their services or to provide entertainment at singing conventions. Few young people had the privilege of receiving formal training in music. Some communities were fortunate enough to have a trained pianist, usually a woman, or a string musician—guitar or fiddle—who taught private lessons to children whose parents insisted that they take them. This was rare and typically found in larger towns that also had schools.

Singing schools were held to teach sacred harp or "shaped note" singing during the seasons that crops were "laid by" and people had free time. From these singing schools, choirs were formed on the spur of the moment to provide music for church services. Many times, a minimally trained deacon or other church leader would occupy the front platform before the preacher arrived and plead with members from the congregation to "come on up and join the choir." These groups often had a handful of people who could read music, but mostly they sang the melody line, following the song leader.

Although a few of the larger city churches had choirs consisting of trained volunteers, for the most part small town and rural churches relied on individuals with much enthusiasm and very little training. Furthermore, there were limited opportunities to receive training. As settlers moved in from more populated areas along the East Coast, they brought their more sophisticated taste in music and expected the churches to provide a more worshipful service.

Enter Donald and Frances Winters. Donald was born to Jacob Oscar and Charlotte Rehmert Winters on December 2, 1910, at the family home in Greenville, Ohio. He grew up a happy child until five years of age when his brother's piano teacher noticed that Donald was playing the piano by ear. At that time, piano teachers traveled to the homes of their students and gave lessons on their pianos. This was true of an old German teacher named Herman Ostheimer, from whom Donald's two older brothers took lessons. The teacher heard one of the assigned pieces being played very well and was ready to commend Donald's older brother when he discovered that it was five-year-old Donald who was playing. After talking with him briefly and hearing him play, Mr. Ostheimer suggested to Donald's mother that it was Donald who should be taking lessons. Thus began a lifelong association of Donald with music.

Donald's interest in music increased, and at age eight he sang Handel's *Messiah* at Christmastime in the Greenville Community Chorus. In 1921, he was elected pianist for the

Sunday School assembly. In 1922, Donald accepted the Lord in the First Christian Church of Greenville, but he insisted on being immersed in the First Baptist Church. Donald obtained his first paid job as organist for the church. His church purchased its first pipe organ, a small German-made Feldgemarker, and Donald became the organist. Although the church organ was his first love, Donald's interests went beyond playing for church and during 1926 and 1927, he was the relief organist at the local theater for silent movies.

During his high school years, he served as organist for his high school, played violin in the school orchestra, and played tuba in the band. The summer following graduation, he went on tour with the Chester Scott company and performed one-night stands in a dozen Midwestern and Western states. In November 1928, following the financial collapse and resulting bankruptcy of the dairy company where Donald's father worked, the Winters family moved to Springfield, Ohio, about 50 miles east. Donald, however, stayed on in Greenville teaching piano lessons, serving as organist for the Christian Church, and playing for silent movies.

The Depression made it difficult for people to pay for piano lessons, and Donald ended up joining the Ohio Lucky Eleven dance band and touring with them for two years, doing mostly one-night stands. Donald soon grew tired of the lifestyle and the ethical and moral values of the band members and the owners of the establishments where the band played. He returned to Springfield, where he moved in with his parents and sought employment. His family had joined Covenant Presbyterian Church, which had a full choir program for all ages. He studied theory and voice with the church music director, Ruth Ingle, and organ with the church organist, Mrs. Ruth D. Whittingdon, on the four-manual Ernest M. Skinner organ. Choir members received free voice lessons in exchange for their commitment to attend rehearsals and performances.

All of these experiences served Donald well as preparation to enter Westminster Choir College of Princeton University. In the fall of 1935, even though he did not have the money for a year of study, he decided to go to Princeton and try to work his way through college. With a fifty-dollar loan from an insurance company, he caught a ride with a trucker and arrived at Princeton with fifteen dollars in his pocket. Although he had not applied for admission in advance, he was accepted and put on a work team in charge of the dish machine in the commons to earn his room and board. During his first summer, Donald remained in school and worked with a grounds crew to mow and trim the expansive campus. He also worked on the cleaning crew to clean out the dorms and get them ready for students to return in the fall. This allowed him to keep up his organ practice throughout the summer months.

Princeton University Chapel

## MUSICAL VESPER SERVICE

Auspices of Princeton University

DECEMBER 17, 1939

Sung by The Westminster Choir College

---

ORDER OF SERVICE

PRELUDE—"How Brightly Shines the Morning Star"        Dietrich Buxtehude
PROCESSIONAL
CALL TO WORSHIP
RESPONSE
VESPER CAROL—134 "The First Noel"                          Traditional Carol
    (*Unannounced—Congregation rising*)
ANTHEM—"Sing We All Noel"                                        Curtis York
SCRIPTURE
PRAYERS—Choral Amen.
ANTHEM—"In Dulci Jubilo"                                    Fourteenth Century
    Arr. F. Melius Christiansen
EVENING CAROL—124, "O Come, All Ye Faithful"
    J. F. Wade's "Cantus Diversi", 1751
    (*Unannounced—Congregation rising*)
THE MEDITATION:
  "Carillon—I Heard the Bells on Christmas Day"        Noble Cain
  "I Sing of a Maiden"                                Fifteenth Century
    Arr. Donald E. Sellew
  "Joseph Came Seeking a Resting Place"            Ernest Willoughby
  "A Rose Breaks into Bloom"                        Johannes Brahms
  "Whence Those Sounds Symphonious"              Charles H. Kitson
  "Hallelujah Chorus"                      George Frederick Handel
SILENT PRAYER
CHORAL RESPONSE
RECESSIONAL HYMN—125, "Hark, the Herald Angels Sing"
    Arr. from Felix Mendelssohn Bartholdy
    (*Congregation and Choir*)
PRAYER AND BENEDICTION
POSTLUDE—"Fugue in C Major"                    Johann Sebastian Bach

---

Princeton University Chapel

## MUSICAL VESPER SERVICE

Auspices of Princeton University

JANUARY 31, 1937

Sung by The Westminster Choir School

---

ORDER OF SERVICE

PRELUDE—Prelude on "How Sinks the Golden Sun"        Bruce Simonds
PROCESSIONAL
CALL TO WORSHIP
SANCTUS
INVOCATION
VESPER HYMN—25, "All Hail the Power of Jesus' Name"        Oliver Holden
    (*Unannounced—Congregation rising*)
ANTHEM—"Lowly Now Before Him Bending"        T. Frederick H. Candlyn
SCRIPTURE
PRAYERS—Choral Response—"Lead Me, Lord"            Samuel S. Wesley
ANTHEM—"The Shadows of Evening Are Falling"        Clarence Dickinson
EVENING HYMN—178, "My Faith Looks Up to Thee"            Lowell Mason
    (*Unannounced—Congregation rising*)
THE MEDITATION:
  "God Is a Spirit"                                David Hugh Jones
  "Hosanna"                                  F. Melius Christiansen
  "Meditation at St. Clotilde"                        Phillip James
  "Come, O Thou Traveller Unknown"                T. Tertius Noble
  "Ho, Every One That Thirsteth"              W. C. MacFarlane
SILENT PRAYER
CHORAL BENEDICTION
RECESSIONAL—"Jerusalem the Golden"                  George F. LeJeune
POSTLUDE—"Toccata"                                        E. S. Barnes

# Donald's Professional Career Begins

In his second year, Donald was placed in a weekend position as organist of First Presbyterian Church of Trenton and earned enough money to pay his personal expenses during that year. He traveled by bus each Sunday from Princeton to Trenton and stayed over on Sunday afternoons at the church. This allowed him to practice on the church organ and to plan for the next Sunday service.

From 1937 to 1941, Donald was placed in the weekend position as organist of the First Presbyterian Church of Englewood, New Jersey. Although a winter-only position, it paid well enough to allow him to save money to cover his expenses. During these years, he worked at the church from Friday noon until Sunday afternoon. The church provided a room in a boarding house for him.

During his years in Englewood, Donald developed three choirs. The adult choir provided music for Sunday morning services and special occasions and rehearsed on Friday evenings. The high school choir rehearsed on Sunday afternoons and sang in the evening services, always singing at least one anthem from memory and joining the adult choir for special occasions. These combined choirs sang *The Messiah* every Christmas. The third choir was made up of junior high boys and girls ages nine to twelve and sang occasionally, always from memory. These choirs grew in size and quality during the four years that Donald was in Englewood.

While working in Springfield with the music program, Donald became acquainted with an older music teacher, Kathryn Scanland, who was also much interested in Westminster Choir College. Donald entered Westminster in 1935 with only high school credits. Kathryn entered in 1936 with a few college hours to transfer. Kathryn was assigned by the college to room with Frances Weaver, who also had college work to transfer, although little of it was in music. Kathryn and Frances were assigned to off-campus housing. Although it was easy walking distance, Kathryn had a car. Donald did not have a car at this time, but he knew his way from New York City to Philadelphia, and he did not mind driving in the heavy traffic between the cities. Kathryn did not like driving in the heavy traffic, and she and Frances often called upon Donald to drive them when they went on excursions outside Princeton.

## A Team is Formed

Thus, Donald and Frances met and were thrown together in class and outside of school, giving them a better opportunity to become acquainted. For the first year and a half, this was merely a friendship, but the relationship began to warm up when they went to the Junior Dance together. In February, they agreed to be married and made plans for a Colorado wedding.

Donald Winters and Frances Weaver were married on June 24, 1940, in the First Presbyterian Church of Greeley, Colorado. Frances was a member of the Baptist church there but was taking voice lessons from the choir director of the Presbyterian church and wanted the choir to sing the "Wedding March" as it was written to be sung. The newly married couple spent two days in Frances' uncle's cabin in the Rockies before they rushed home to be in Marion, Virginia for the next Sunday service.

Donald lacked one year to complete course work for his master's degree, even though he had already presented his master recital in organ. They had a small furnished apartment and drove back and forth to classes. Frances was secretary to Mrs. Williamson, who was academic dean.

In the fall of 1940, Donald and Frances both submitted their resumes to the placement office at Westminster Choir College, hoping to find work to begin right away. Among the questions asked was, "Where and in what denomination do you wish to work?" Frances answered, "Anywhere except the South." Donald answered, "Any church except a Baptist." The year passed with no good leads. After returning from the spring tour, they had no offers, and they went to the placement office and withdrew their objections. Within a week, they were contacted by Dr. Ellis A. Fuller of the First Baptist Church of Atlanta, who wanted to discuss a full church-wide music program. He invited them to come to Atlanta that weekend at the church's expense. The visit was made to Atlanta and the offer was extended and accepted. The couple began their work in Atlanta in June 1941, beginning with Vacation Bible School.

## A Remarkable Step

Priority was given that first summer to planning, attending conferences, and consulting with the educational leadership of the church to assure that the music program supported the overall program. The second priority was to develop a high school choir. The high school choir was organized in time to begin leading the music for the evening service the Sunday after Labor Day. That same Sunday morning, the adult choir sang two anthems, one from memory. This was the actual beginning of the graded music program.

That summer, a detailed plan took place with Dr. Fuller for the entire program. Brochures where printed and distributed to educate the church on the plan. The pastor's paragraph in the weekly church bulletin was used to promote the plan, and it was introduced to the Atlanta community through articles in the *Atlanta Constitution*.

**astor's aragraphs**

**A New Era** Every church leader feels very keenly the responsibility to enlist the young people for active participation in the work of the church. Music offers a glorious opportunity for the realization of this worthy purpose. Everybody loves music. Nearly everyone has some musical talent. Music has been through the ages a voice of praise unto God. It is a peculiar language for the utterance of emotions that the tongue cannot possibly describe. For that reason every church should make the maximum use of music in a church-wide effort to deepen the spirituality of the people and to inspire church-wide participation in worship.

The Westminster Plan of Music, which we have adopted for this church and which we are today inaugurating, was conceived and developed with exactly this end in view. If the plan is worked successfully, it will accomplish two ends without fail, namely, it will develop a consciousness and use of music which no other plan can achieve, and it will enlist the greatest number of people to a vital interest in the church and in an actual participation in its program.

Dr. John Finley Williamson, President of the Westminster Choir College, after studying our church building thoroughly and learning something of the personnel of our membership, stated that within a few years we ought to have at least five hundred people enlisted in the department of music of our church.

The purpose of this program is to discover the musical talent in the church, to enlist it, to train it, and to use it. In this way we can make it glorify God and at the same time lead our people to new heights of spirituality.

Today Mr. and Mrs. Donald Winters begin their work with us. No couple could possibly receive a higher recommendation than Dr. Williamson gave them. Both of them are thoroughly trained and consecrated. Mr. Winters has a Master's degree in organ and a Bachelor's degree in voice, both from the Westminster Choir College. He has had broad and varied experience both as a singer and as an organist. Mrs. Winters has her Bachelor's degree in voice from the Westminster Choir College and also a Bachelor's degree in religious education from Denison University.

Mr. Winters will serve as organist and choir director. Mrs. Winters will assist him in every possible way. She will contribute her voice to the adult choir and will work with Mr. Winters in developing the several choruses which they will organize and train as rapidly as possible.

Surely our parents will respond enthusiastically in co-operating with Mr. and Mrs. Winters in building a great musical organization in our church; for the entire program is designed in the interest of those whom God has endowed with musical gifts.

We certainly want to maintain a great adult choir. We want all that we now have supplemented by just as many other singers as we can bring into the choir loft. Mr. Winters will give voice lessons without cost to the members of the adult choir with the understanding that their only obligation will be the giving of their services by singing in the choir.

We will want a young people's choir and an intermediate choir and a junior choir and perhaps a choir for children of even younger age. This is not an outline of what we are committing to the Winters as a program. They are our leaders. We will depend upon them to direct us in creating such organizations as will promote their program.

We pledge to them our heartiest and most prayerful co-operation that this musical plan may contribute to our church what we know it has contributed to scores of other churches throughout the land.

**Singers** We believe that the coming of Mr. and Mrs. Winters means far more than the developing of a great chorus choir to lead us in our worship periods. It should mean, and I dare say will mean, that some of our young people will be influenced to yield their lives for the type of service that they are doing in building the Kingdom of God upon earth. We have young men and young women to whom God has given rich gifts, who, if aided in developing those gifts, will be exceedingly valuable to the Kingdom of God. For that reason we are anxious for every person in the church who has a voice that should be developed for definite service in the Kingdom to apply at once to Mr. Winters for a position in the adult choir. Of course, in a great church-wide undertaking of this sort we must leave the whole program in the hands of the man upon whom we have placed the responsibility. Great indeed it will be in the lives of our singers and the families that they represent and the church at large if we can use music as a definite means of enriching our fellowship with one another and with God.

**THE WESTMINSTER PLAN**

On next Wednesday evening, July 16, at the regular prayer meeting hour, Mr. and Mrs. Winters will discuss in detail the Westminster Plan of Music which we have inaugurated for our church.

They will go into a detailed discussion of the plan with the view of informing our people concerning just what it means, what it will do for our church, and what will be necessary to accomplish the ends to which it is committed.

I am anxious for every member to attend this service. They will have a full and frank word in regard to the technique of enlisting our boys and girls for this service. I am sure that parents, who are cognizant of the great problems they face in connection with the spiritual lives of their children, will seize upon this opportunity to increase their interest in the church and thereby fortify themselves against the assaults of the Wicked One whose one purpose is to destroy.

There are many things which the mothers themselves can do. Mr. and Mrs. Winters will tell us what these things are.

I am anxious for the entire membership to know that the Westminster Plan is not merely a scheme to develop an evangelistic chorus. It is a musical educational program for the spiritual benefit of those who are enlisted in the choirs and for the benefit of those who will worship under the leadership of these choirs. It is a tremendous program. Let us see it and work with it in order that the full blessing may come to our church.

The idea took hold, and in a very short time, a full program was installed with the following components:

The Cherub Choir - ages 4-6      The Canto Choir - ages 6-8

The Carol Choir - ages 9-11 girls      The Crusader Choir - ages 9-11 boys

The Celestial Choir - ages 12-14 girls      The Challenger Choir - ages 12-14 boys

The Chapel Choir - senior high school boys and girls by audition

This model was known as the "Westminster Plan," and it was heralded in church publications and the *Atlanta*

The Chancel Choir (adults), First Baptist Church, Atlanta, autumn, 1941.

*Constitution* as the first fully comprehensive music program in any Baptist church in Georgia, and any church of any denomination in the Atlanta area. The success of this plan at First Atlanta drew representatives from throughout the South who wanted to emulate it in their home churches. Although the Winterses were very reluctant to claim that they were the first to implement this plan in the Southern Baptist Convention, many church historians have given them credit for it. At the same time that they were establishing the program in Atlanta, Southwestern Baptist Theological Seminary in Fort Worth, Texas was promoting a similar concept in Southern Baptist Churches in the Southwest.

**WINTERS**

## DONALD WINTERS, Conductor

Mr. Winters, formerly minister of music at the First Baptist Church, Atlanta, Georgia, is a graduate of Westminster Choir College, Princeton, New Jersey, where he was a member of the famous Westminster Choir during his student years. He studied voice with Dr. John Finley Williamson, president of Westminster Choir College, and also majored in organ, studying with Dr. Carl Weinrich, the organ virtuoso.

## *What They Say About the Choir...*

"I was profoundly impressed not only with the skill and finesse of Professor Winters and the members of the choir but with their sincerity and spirit of consecration in the service and in all their contacts with our church people. They certainly created much good will for the Seminary. I only hope that I shall have the privilege again of having this choir in my church."
—CARROLL HUBBARD, PASTOR
First Baptist Church, Ashland, Kentucky

". . . appreciate greatly your giving us the opportunity of having the Choir on our campus. Its visit is another evidence of the close relationships that have existed through the years between the Seminary and the University of Richmond." —GEORGE M. MODLIN, PRESIDENT
The University of Richmond, Richmond, Va.

"The music loving people of Danville and Centre College heard the choir and were all of the opinion that a great program was given."
—R. R. COUEY, PASTOR
Lexington Avenue Baptist Church, Danville, Kentucky

". . . If the program which they presented in Greenville last night is a sample of the type of church music to which the Louisville school aspires, a new and superior conception of the role of music in the worship service has been inspired.
"It augers well for the future of church music, for the dignity of its place in religion, for the beauty which it brings to daily living, and for the faith which it expresses in God and man."
—ELEANOR BARTON
The Greenville (S. C.) Piedmont

"The program made a definite contribution to the spiritual development of our community."
—PRIMITIVO DELGADO, PASTOR
Marion (Va.) Baptist Church

"The Seminary Choir made a profound impression on the city of Lynchburg and the surrounding areas. The evening in sacred music was indeed an experience of worship."
—WARNER EARLE FUSSELLE, PASTOR
Rivermont Avenue Baptist Church
Lynchburg, Virginia

"It was a joy to have the choir with our church. They made a most enviable impression, not only with our church, but with music lovers of other churches. I am sure I am safe in saying that no musical group ever appeared in any church during my pastorates that more graciously endeared itself to the church, nor gave a better account of itself musically than did this choir."
—E. GIBSON DAVIS, PASTOR
First Baptist Church
Kingsport, Tenn.

"It was indeed a blessing to our congregation to have the Seminary Choir in our church in May. The service was even more than one could have anticipated. We appreciate the rare privilege that was ours to share with you in this great work. Many of us were particularly impressed by the excellent program that had been prepared for the service. It was indeed one of real worship." —T. RUPERT COLEMAN, PASTOR
Ginter Park Baptist Church
Richmond, Virginia

"This program has one of the finest formats of any religious music program it has been our pleasure to hear. It is most effective in that the message of the Bible is transmitted in capsule form, and with the added impetus of the beautiful music, the program is even more forceful. . . ."
—DAVID B. HIGHBAUGH,
Program Director
Radio Station WHIR
Danville, Kentucky

"The service was marked by a striking combination of reverence and artistic effectiveness in the sphere of music."
—THE CHARLOTTE (N. C.) OBSERVER

... **MEMORIAL CHAPEL**

"A splendid organization that had wonderful quality of tone ... virility ... and dynamic range."
—W. HINES SIMS,
Sunday School Board,
Southern Baptist Convention.

## KENNETH POOL, Organist

Mr. Pool is a graduate of Furman University, Greenville, South Carolina, and the University of Michigan School of Music, where he was a student of the late Palmer Christian, organist. He also has done graduate study at Eastman School of Music and at the Organ Institute, Andover, Massachusetts.

In the two years the Winterses were in Atlanta, all choirs except kindergarten were organized and provided music for Sunday evening services from time to time. During this time, two Christmas vespers services, the

Easter presentation of "The Seven Last Words of Christ" by Dubois with harp and organ, and a patriotic service were the most memorable. Due to the success of these special programs, churches from throughout the South wanted similar programs.

The program also had a strong influence on Southern Baptist churches. Early in 1942, the Sunday School Board of the Southern Baptist Convention sent Dr. Allen Graves to study the program. He spent a week interviewing church staff, deacons, members of the choir, Sunday School and training leaders, and parents of the children. Dr. Graves returned to Nashville and wrote *Let Us Sing*, which was published by the board. It was widely circulated and led churches throughout the Southern Baptist Convention to initiate comprehensive music programs.

In the spring of 1942, Dr. Ellis Fuller was elected President of Southern Baptist Theological Seminary in Louisville, Kentucky. Dr. Fuller always said he was conscripted because he did not want to leave the pastorate.

One of Dr. Fuller's first priorities was to build a school of church music at Southern Seminary to train musicians for the churches of the Southern Baptist Convention. During the winter of 1942-43, when Ellis Fuller was president of SBTS, he spoke with some of his trustees about his desire to build a school of church musicians along with missionaries and all other positions in the church. Not all the seminary faculty were enthusiastic over the proposal, but one of the local trustees purchased a house adjacent to the seminary and donated it for a school of music. Dr. Fuller contacted the Winterses, and they had several conversations about them coming to Southern Seminary. Donald and Frances did not feel that it was wise for them to move at that time. Dr. Fuller continued to share with them his dream and that he must decide how he would use the property that he had been given. He was increasingly insistent because he did not think there was anyone else who could do what he wanted done. Unfortunately, Donald had been drafted into the United States Army.

## On to Seminary

Donald and Frances accepted the position, despite Donald being drafted, and Frances, who was pregnant, moved to Louisville. She began planning, writing curriculum, and teaching the few classes that the seminary had in place. Fortunately, the seminary paid to move her to Louisville. Donald's sister, Mary, came down from Ohio to drive them to Louisville and helped Frances settle into the apartment that had been provided for them.

Donald was inducted into the Army at Fort McPherson near Atlanta, and he remained there for the next few months. After a period in McPherson, Donald was transferred to New York. Finally, he was assigned to the post chapel, Schofield Barracks, Honolulu, where he was assigned as a clerk because he could type. He was granted a three-day pass so he could participate in the dedication of Cooke Hall, the new home of the school of music, and while in Louisville he shared in the recital for the dedication of the new organ. This was his only contact with the seminary.

During Donald's years in the Army, Frances and Gene, their firstborn son, remained in Louisville, where Frances gave all her time to launching the new school of church music. For the first two years, they lived in the music building, and Dr. Fuller assigned a student couple to live with them to take care of the apartment, cook, and care for Gene in exchange for room and board.

In the year 1944-45, the girls of the music school lived upstairs in Cooke Hall. During the 1945-46 year, the girls moved to the new Barnard Hall, across Buena Vista from Cooke Hall. Donald served as consultant, and every aspect of the new school was discussed in detail in the daily letters that were exchanged with Frances during his Army years.

When Donald returned, he began teaching immediately with the opening of the second quarter. A third practice pipe organ had been added, as well as a number of pianos. A grand piano had been given the first year and three additional grand pianos, along with a number of upright pianos, were added for the practice rooms.

Donald took over the seminary choir, inviting seminary students to audition in order to fill out all the sections. The male sections were low because of the draft. In addition, Donald taught conducting, vocal pedagogy, and a very heavy schedule of private lessons. The spring of that year, they took their first choir tour, going all the way to Miami and singing concerts in churches every night. In Miami, the choir sang at the Southern Baptist Convention, giving them much good publicity. The choir soon built a fine reputation which made recruiting much easier.

On campus, the choir sang at each of the chapel services, but became known in the community for the vespers services, which were held once a month on Sunday afternoons between Thanksgiving and Easter. These services consisted of music, spoken parts, and scripture. Seminary professors were frequently asked to preside and to read the scripture passages.

Dr. Fuller's foremost project was to construct a seminary chapel. At Dr. Fuller's request, Donald Winters took charge of designing the chapel organ. Donald began his suggestions for the organ while still in Hawaii, and when he was discharged and returned to the seminary campus, he took the lead. Many people had input, especially the organ builder, but Donald assumed the major role in designing the four-manual Aeolean-Skinner organ that was provided but not installed until the fall of 1950. Unfortunately, one of the first occasions for the organ to be used was Dr. Fuller's funeral. The special organ required much in design for the building, and so Donald became the chief person, working with the architects, in designing the chapel.

Donald believed that the success of the program was dependent on outreach. A first in the way of performance for the music program was a series of short radio broadcasts known as the "Voices of Praise." Outreach was felt also in the numerous choral festivals Donald was invited to lead.

The many problems of getting the school of music started are told in a paper Donald presented to the entire seminary family in chapel on Founder's Day, 1976.

After the death of Dr. Fuller, Duke McCall became President of Southern Baptist Seminary. Dr. McCall did not support Donald as Dr. Fuller had and began to maneuver to replace him as head of the newly created music school. Donald and Frances made the decision to resign from the seminary and return to Bloomington, Indiana, to Indiana State University so Donald could pursue a Ph.D. in music. Donald desired to obtain a degree in church music, but the National Association of Schools of Music (NASM), the accrediting agency for music degree programs, had not approved a doctoral degree in either church music or applied music. His advisor suggested that he switch to music education. Although he had already completed all coursework for a Ph.D., including all required proficiencies in English, French, German, and voice, and an inside minor in organ and outside minor in philosophy, he took the dean's advice and switched to music education. A new head of the music education department had come to Indiana State, and he made it so difficult for majors that not a single one completed the degree in the four-year time period. Seeing the handwriting on the wall, Donald decided to move on with his life.

Living in Bloomington was good for the family. Both boys participated in the scouting program, took piano lessons from an instructor at I.U., and took part in the swimming program. Gene was the most competitive and did quite well as a swimmer.

With the decision to forego his Ph.D. and move ahead with his life and career, early in 1956 Donald submitted his resume to the I.U. placement office for teaching positions. He had few leads but did consider Georgetown College; however, he was not pleased with their plans to name alternate heads of the department to share the position in alternate years. Another offer was from William Jewell College, where music was only offered as a cultural requirement.

In the spring of 1956, Dr. I. E. Rouse, then president of William Carey College in Hattiesburg, Mississippi, called to ask Donald and Frances to meet him at the airport in Indianapolis between flights so that he could conduct an interview for possible employment. Dr. Rouse offered Donald the position of chairman of the division of fine arts at the college and stressed that he wanted to begin offering training in church music, which at that time was not offered at any institution in Mississippi.

The salary was not very attractive, Donald had no financial cushion to fall back on, and he knew nothing about the college. Investigation turned up negative information. The board was debating whether or not to close the school. The same question had been raised four years earlier, but Dr. Rouse had persuaded the board to change from an all-women's college to a co-educational school and to eventually change its name. This change happened in 1952, and the first year, still under the name of Woman's College, it turned out a winning football team. The college experienced growth, but the expenses of an expanded athletic program and constructing a new men's dormitory left it deep in debt.

Dr. Rouse did not admit it, but his health was declining, and it turned out that he had a brain tumor that had caused erratic behavior on his part. He was dismissed by the board, and the dean, Dr. J. Ralph Noonkester, became the youngest college president in the country. Ralph Noonkester had sung in the Southern Seminary chorus under Donald Winters for four years, and his wife Naomi was a graduate of the SBTS School of Music. They were both interested in offering training in church music.

## Their Destiny

In June 1956, Donald began receiving letters and telegrams from church and college people congratulating him on becoming head of Carey's fine arts program. These, along with a clipping from the Hattiesburg newspaper announcing that he had been appointed to that position, was the first that Donald knew of it, since he had not yet said that he would come. With no other offers on the table and his finances depleted, he accepted the college's offer to pay his moving expenses. The Winters family moved to Hattiesburg in the middle of August 1956.

They arrived on a weekend with the temperature standing at 104 degrees, and they moved into a house at 1401

Vernon Street, two blocks from the campus. The house had no insulation and was up on blocks without a foundation. With no air conditioning, the family was soaking wet the entire weekend. If there had been any place else to go, or any money to go on, the family probably would not have stayed.

Saturday, Oct. 22, 1966   Hattiesburg AMERICAN   Page 9

## Church music program unique at Carey College

William Carey College is one of the few Southern Baptist colleges that offers a complete and adequate church music program for potential church musicians. This is a unique degree program that has been in existence at Carey for the past 10 years under the leadership of Donald Winters, chairman of the Fine Arts Dept.

The studies offered are so complete that they fully prepare the student for full-time church music work without additional graduate study. Further study in a seminary, of course, is most desirable for many students, but the Carey chuch music course is a professional course in itself rather than preprofessional preparation.

It includes several specialized courses in the history and literature of church music, church music education and methods, the administration of a fully-graded choir program, conducting and applied techniques, and music in worship and evangelism along with core subjects in basic musicianship and applied concentration in organ, piano, or voice.

"Approximately 90 per cent of the church music majors at Carey College are employed in part-time positions in church music during their college years. This helps in the earning of their college expenses and gives valuable experience in their chosen field," Mr. Winters said.

Every single church music graduate, who has wished to be placed in church music positions upon graduation, has found such employment readily.

Carey's other major area of music training is in the field of music teaching. According to nationwide surveys the large majority of openings in the music area are in these two fields. The curriculum for the bachelor of music degree in music education meets all requirements for Mississippi state certification in public school music. And what is even more important — it meets the core requirements of the college itself for general liberal arts studies so essential to the educated individual.

During the past seven years, 100 per cent of Carey's music education graduates who have desired placement have been placed in music - teaching positions.

## Objectives of Carey Music Dept.

The objectives of the Department of Music at William Carey College are four-fold: to offer every student an opportunity for acquaintance with music as one area of general culture, and for training and participation in this area; to give intensive professional training to students who choose to specialize in performing or teaching and to prepare them for advanced professional training; to prepare teachers and supervisors of music in stateapproved curricula for public schools; and to train for music leadership in Christian service.

In the past 10-year period, 38 percent of the graduates of the department have gone on to graduate study, and 95 percent have been employed professionally in the areas of their specialties. Approximately 30 percent of the general student body each year enrolls in one of several courses in the fine arts area provided for rounding out the liberal arts studies emphasized by the college.

In addition to its course offerings, the music department offers many cultural opportunities to its students and provides which students may gain planning and performing experiences both on and off the campus.

# The Winterses' Career in Hattiesburg

The beginnings in Hattiesburg were not easy. The previous division head had secured a position at Mississippi Southern College, also in Hattiesburg, and he took the best of the Carey music students with him. Thus, Donald inherited a program with only five majors, three of them who could not sing on pitch. There were few offerings in art and only a course or two in theater.

Mississippi Woman's College, the precursor of William Carey College, had always put strong emphasis on the fine arts, especially music and drama. When the school became co-educational, this emphasis did not diminish, but rather took on different directions. When Donald came to Carey in September 1956 as head of the division of fine arts, more emphasis was placed on music. The division of fine arts had two branches, art and music, although there was no major in art. In 1965-66, the division was no longer designated as such. There was a department of music, and the art courses were distributed among other departments. Donald was listed as the head of the department of music. In 1970, the department became the Carey College School of Music with Donald as its dean. At this time the school of music was one of three academic divisions of the college: the school of music, the school of nursing, and the college of arts and sciences. Schools of education and business were added later.

On December 4, 1984, at a banquet and presentation of *The Messiah,* the school was officially named the Donald and Frances Winters School of Music at William Carey College.

Beginning in 1957, the objectives of music study at William Carey College were fourfold: to offer students an opportunity to become acquainted with music as an area of general culture; to give intensive professional training for students who chose to specialize in this area and to prepare them for advanced training; to prepare teachers and supervisors of music for the public schools; and to train for music leadership roles in churches and other areas of service.

In 1956, there were five faculty members, none of whom had a doctoral degree. It was always Donald's desire to have a stable faculty, yet changes are inevitable, especially when opportunities for advancement in status and salary are presented. From 1957 to 1979, the college had thirty-six faculty members, including adjuncts, some who stayed only a year, especially wives of USM faculty members who moved on. As far as curriculum, during the very first year, Donald set up a new series of curricular plans following the requirements of the National Association of Schools of Music (NASP), knowing there was much to be accomplished before consideration could be given to preparing an application for accreditation. He always planned well ahead so that he would be ready when the opportunity for advancement occurred. This is why, fourteen years later, music was the only department in the college that was ready when the opportunity came for the college to offer a graduate degree. From the beginning, Donald had set up a new and comprehensive record system similar to the one used at Indiana University where Frances had worked in the dean's office.

In 1957-58, Donald set up a Bachelor of Music degree with a major in Church Music, the only one in Mississippi at that time. This degree was considered unique among Southern colleges because of its complete offerings in preparation for full time church music work. In 1973-74, Donald led Carey College to be the first in Mississippi to offer a degree in music therapy, in keeping with his goal of providing graduates who were able to meet unmet needs. During Dr. Winters' tenure, it was the only program in music therapy in the state.

In 1966, the school had its first provisional examination for accreditation by the National Association of Schools of Music, and in 1968 was given full accreditation by that body with a commendation "for the excellence in the music program." In 1978, the status of full accreditation by that body was extended.

In 1970, the first master's degree program in music at any Baptist college in the state was offered at Carey.

Facilities at Carey College were greatly improved during Donald's tenure. In 1956, all music classes were taught on the third floor of Tatum Court administration building, to the dissatisfaction of all concerned. The only exception was in the evening after dinner when students were practicing with all the windows open, and individuals walking around campus could enjoy piano, voice, violin, and other music flowing from "the court."

In the early 1960s, plans began to be formulated for a fine arts building. An unusually hot graduation ceremony in the auditorium of Tatum Court convinced the trustees that the new fine arts building should have a large, air-conditioned auditorium that could accommodate all of the college's needs. Funds for the building were raised in the 1963 development program and the $700,000 Carey Fine Arts Center was finally dedicated on October 23, 1966. Donald and the music faculty had a great deal of input into the early planning, and the final building was a result of collaboration with architects, building consultants, and deans of other schools regarding the outlay and space requirements. It was imperative to have comfortable rooms with high enough ceilings to accommodate sound levels, as well as a provision for offices and storage. This building included Carey's 1,200-seat auditorium, with the largest stage in South Mississippi, faculty offices, seven teaching studios, 36 practice rooms with 30 practice pianos, two practice organs, two listening rooms, a recording room, three classrooms, and dressing and service areas.

In addition to major instruments, a number of string and wind instruments were added for instrumental classes, including two tympani, a representative range of elementary instruments, and rhythm instruments. Also added were overhead, opaque, slide, and movie projectors, all for classroom use. Provisions had been made to make a wall in the largest classroom a projection wall.

Another critical asset that made the music program a success was the support of the Rouse Library. The holdings grew consistently through the years and consisted of books, periodicals, journals, pamphlets, scores, manuscripts, recordings, and multiple copies of music. Listening tables with six outlets were set up in the library.

In January 1971, the School of Music acquired the private collection of Clarence and Helen Dickinson, late founders and professors of Union Seminary School of Music. This unusual collection of books, music, scores, and manuscripts, as well as Dickinson memorabilia, is housed in the Dickinson Room of the Rouse Library. It contains a number of religious folk songs discovered throughout Europe, songs that had never been arranged or published before. The texts were translated by Helen and recorded in manuscripts by the Dickinsons. Included also were some very rare volumes, such as a 1560 copy of the famous Genevan Psalter. Many valuable books from the library of Dr. George Litch Knight, pastor of the Lafayette Avenue Presbyterian Church in Brooklyn, New York, who assisted Carey College with the acquisition of the collection, are also among its treasures. Personal copies of the Dickinsons' own books and compositions, both organ and choral works, and a manuscript copy of Clarence's only opera are there, along with some of their furniture and pictures and items belonging to the poetess Emily Dickinson, a cousin of Dr. Dickinson.

In September 1956, only five music majors were enrolled at Carey College. Ten years later, in 1965-66, the undergraduate enrollment in music was 103, with 83 majors and 20 minors. A summary of the decade indicated that Carey College had graduated 88 degrees in music to 83 students, five students earning both the BA and BS degrees. Forty percent had gone on to further graduate study and 95 percent were employed in professional positions in music.

In the next ten years, the enrollment continued to grow. In 1976-77, there were 131 undergraduate students and 19 graduate students, for a total of 150 enrolled in music.

During Donald's tenure at Carey, student chapters of the following organizations were formed: the Mississippi Education Association, the Student Education Association, Alpha Lambda honor society, Delta Omicron and Phi Mu Alpha national music honoraries for women and men, the Music Educators National Conference, and the Association of Church Musicians. Although no official chapters of the National Guild of Organists or the Hymn Society of America were established, there were members of these prestigious organizations in the faculty and student body.

In 1956, Donald opened the choir to anyone in the small student body (about two hundred students) who would audition for it. Relying on his experience at Marion, Virginia, of teaching everything needed to everyone in the choir, he ended the first year with a very acceptable choir, and it continued to grow in quality and reputation as long as he was at the school. The chorale was his chief contribution to the students and to the school. Through it, the students learned about the choral work most of them would be doing, and through it the college became better known. The school's best publicity at home and on tours, its athletic teams and the touring choir became national competitors. The chorale averaged 45 singers, with the largest being 55 and the smallest 36. These came from all the Southeastern states and as far away as Connecticut, Illinois, Pennsylvania, Colorado, Montana, and New York. Added to these were singers from Switzerland, Hawaii, Argentina, and Japan. This group, under Donald's direction, sang well over 350 performances, with repeat performances in many places. They were invited to be the featured singers on many occasions throughout the Southern Baptist Convention, including six appearances at the Mississippi Baptist State Convention, the Mississippi Federation of Music Clubs state convention, the W.M.U. national convention, several appearances at the annual Southern Baptist Convention, and the Southern Baptist Music Conference. In addition, the chorale sang at dozens of local civic clubs, church events, youth rallies, workshops, the Union Music Festival, and the American Musicological Society national convention.

The chorale premiered several works of Carey composers, including Robert Gauldin's Christmas cantata *Herod and the Maji,* Charles Endsley's setting of *The Lord's Prayer,* and several choral works of Benjamin Dunford. The chorale tour program was unique in that it was set up

School Of Music
WILLIAM CAREY COLLEGE
Hattiesburg, Mississippi

An example of Chorale
tour programs.This
tour was the only one
to go outside the U.S.

FIFTEENTH ANNUAL TOUR

of the

CAREY COLLEGE CHORALE

Donald Winters, Conductor

1970 - 1971

> The Carey College Chorale is recognized as one of the outstanding performing choirs in the nation. Repeatedly it has won acclaim throughout the South and East where concerts have been presented before numberless churches, schools, civic clubs, conventions, and music organizations.
>
> Dr. Donald Winters, conductor of the Chorale, is also administrative head of the William Carey College School of Music. Under his 15 years of leadership the music program of the school has become one of the most respected among all private colleges in the area. The calibre of the music faculty, the spaciousness of the facilities, and the academic program have provided the School of Music with justification this school year, 1970-1971, to begin graduate programs in two major areas—music education and church music.
>
> In addition to the master's degree, the school offers the bachelor degree in music with concentration in a variety of areas. The College also offers bachelor degrees in the arts and sciences in every major academic area of study.
>
> The Carey School of Music is a member of the National Association of Schools of Music. More detailed information concerning any phase of the William Carey College program may be obtained upon request.

as a worship service rather than a succession of numbers. There were brief scripture readings throughout to tie the music together into a theme. The service always ended with the "Benediction" by Peter C. Lutkin, and William Carey graduates in the audience were invited to stand during this benediction. Graduates of the Carey School of Music joined in the singing of this familiar hymn. People all over the South remarked about the unusual format and how meaningful the service was. Almost always the program included a Bach Motet because Donald believed that this repertory was best for building voices and sectional unity. Always they were memorized. It was also a part of his belief that professional musicians should be acquainted with great music. Not only was this stressed with the singing groups but also in his literature classes.

The oratorio choir was also under Donald's direction. This group was comprised of the entire student body of the school of music, including some faculty, plus any among the Carey students who chose to elect this activity. This group sang one major work each year. Usually, this was a sacred work with organ accompaniment, but small instrumental ensembles were also frequently used. The group joined forces with the theater department to produce Menotti's *Amahl and the Night Visitors* and again for the light opera *The Princess and the Pea*. Sacred works included standard oratorio repertory, but some selections not so often heard included Handel's *Israel in Egypt, Gloria* by Antonio Vivaldi, the Saint-Saens' *Christmas Oratorio, Jeptha* by Carissmi, *Behold the Lamb of God* by T. W. Dean, as well as *The Creation* by Haydn and *A German Requiem* (Brahms) for which he brought to Carey the well-known bass soloist David Ford from Nashville.

The oratorio choir appeared with two major symphony orchestras in concert: the New Orleans Symphony Orchestra under the direction of Werner Torkanowsky singing the Verdi *Te Daum Laudimus*, and the Mobile Symphony Orchestra directed by James Yestadt when Bach's *St. Matthew Passion* was sung in Mobile and in Hattiesburg. Two student winners of state contests also appeared with the Jackson Symphony under the direction of Lewis Dalvit.

# The Clarion-Ledger

*Mississippi's Leading Newspaper For More Than A Century*

AP Leased Wires — Wirephoto   JACKSON, MISSISSIPPI, WEDNESDAY, OCTOBER 18, 1967   VOL. CXXIX, NO. 252

LOOK OVER MUSIC — William Carey College Choral members look over music with director Donald Winters in preparation for a performance with the New Orleans Philharmonic Symphony Orchestra, Friday, Oct. 20. Students Hank Guest of Jackson; Cheryl Watts of Zurich, Switzerland; and Mary Bollinger of Stark, Fla., shared in the intense practice sessions involving the 80-voice choral group. The concert begins at 8:30 p.m. in Thomas Hall Auditorium.

The only time during the Winters' tenure that Carey College publicity appeared in color on the front page of the state's leading newspaper in Mississippi.

Donald arranged for the Carey School of Music to sponsor a number of special choral workshops for the benefit of Carey music students and Carey graduates with their high school choirs as well as music teachers and church musicians from the surrounding area. For these, he brought in outstanding directors, teachers, clinicians, and choreographers. These included Dr. John Finley Williamson, Dr. Buryl Red, Dr. Phillip

Landgrave, Dr. Elaine Brown, Ragan Courtney, and Grace Courtney, among others. Winters also introduced youth *musicales* to South Mississippi when they were first made available. These were not always well received at first by older members of congregations, who were not used to contemporary sounds, new movements, and new forms, but they were immediately popular with the young people. Such works as *Celebrate Life* (Buryl Red) and *Bright New Wings* (Ragan Courtney) were introduced to the area by the Carey Chorale.

An important event in 1973, instigated by Donald and sponsored by the Carey School of Music, was the centenary celebration of the birth of noted church musician, Clarence Dickinson. This was scheduled to coincide with the dedication of the Dickinson Library, which Donald and Frances had been instrumental in getting for Carey College. This event brought to the campus important musicians from New York to California and gave the college some of its best publicity. This festival was designated by the American Guild of Organists, of which Dickinson was a founding member, as the official centenary in the country, and was covered by staff reporters of the major music magazines. In addition to honoring the memory of the Drs. Dickinson, it also reviewed the 100 years of American music, especially in the field of organ and church music. Papers were given by outstanding recognized musicians, musicologists, and authors.

Blue Mountain College in Blue Mountain, Mississippi, recognized the outstanding contributions of Donald Winters to church music throughout the Southern Baptist Convention by conferring on him the honorary degree, *Doctor of Music,* on May 11, 1970. Donald had completed all requirements, including recitals and research, for the doctoral degree at Indiana University, but due to the death of his doctoral committee chair and the confusion which followed, he was never able to receive the degree. This conferral was perhaps one of the most meaningful recognitions of his life.

In 1979, Donald retired as dean of the School of Music, although he remained as a member of the faculty for two more years and was given the title *Senior Professor of Music.* At his retirement, he was designated as Professor Emeritus.

Upon his retirement, Donald received accolades from numerous sources, including the City of Hattiesburg, First Baptist Church of Hattiesburg, the music department of the Mississippi Baptist Convention, the Southern Baptist Music Conference, the American Guild of Organists, the Hattiesburg Community Concert Board, Southern Baptist Seminary, the Choral Conductors Guild of America, the Outstanding Educators of America, the Rotary Foundation of Rotary International, and Omicron Delta Kappa.

Numerous activities were planned for Donald's retirement, and he composed a letter expressing his sincere gratitude and summarizing his life and accomplishments. All who knew Frances Winters knew that she was the power behind Donald, and she deserves as much praise as he. The last official act by the William Carey College Board of Trustees made this clear when the board approved the renaming of the School of Music to the Donald and Frances Winters School of Music. The event was recorded by the local newspaper, *The Hattiesburg American*: "A legacy was immortalized  on Sept. 4 when William Carey College trustees, upon the recommendation of the president, J. Ralph Noonkester, voted to name the school of music at the college The Donald and Frances Winters School of Music. From humble beginnings in 1958, Donald and Frances guided the program to national imminence, to school status, and developed the first graduate-level degree program, The Masters of Music."

The legacy of Donald and Frances Winters lives on in the lives of the students that they have trained and continues to be handed down to those who are influenced by them. The Winters Chair of Music and the Donald and Frances Winters School of Music at William Carey University will stand as a monument to their accomplishments.

This compilation of historical documents, recollections of students, and accomplishments of Donald and Frances Winters is intended to preserve their legacy. The Winterses spent their entire professional career at three locations: two years at FBC Atlanta, six years at Southern Baptist Theological Seminary, and nearly three decades at William Carey College (now University). They left indelible footprints at every place they served. In Atlanta, they created the first fully graded choir program in any church in Georgia, and perhaps in the Southern Baptist Convention. They established the School of Church Music at Southern Baptist Theological Seminary in Louisville, Kentucky. Their greatest accomplishment was at William Carey College, where they started from almost nothing and built a nationally recognized choral program. When they arrived at Carey, the former chair of the music department had departed to a larger public university and had taken all his better students, leaving only five majors. The Winterses started at that point and built a program that claimed yearly 150 majors and minors. During their stay they obtained full accreditation by the National Association of Schools of Music (NASM), established the first graduate degree at William Carey and the first graduate degree in Church Music at any college in the state. Their legacy lives on in the lives of many of their students who continue to serve throughout the country.

While Donald was the face of the program, Frances was the strong, silent backbone who provided the support for their success. Her quiet, gracious manner was evident in the organized programs and curricula. Students who had a class under Frances remember her as among their finest teachers.

It is our prayer that this effort will keep their legacy alive for posterity.

## Reminiscences of Donald and Frances Winters

## Appendix I
## Josephine D'Arpa

An example of Donald and Frances Winters' nurturing and developing students is Miss Josephine D'Arpa. Born to a pastor and his wife in Miami, her father took her as a child to various churches, homeless shelters, and other gatherings and stood her on a chair where she would sing for the people. At the age of nine, she accepted Christ as her savior. When she graduated from high school, Josephine dedicated her life to full time Christian service and enrolled in the University of Tampa to pursue music as a degree. Her minister of music knew that she needed to go where she would grow in her skills of music. He remembered his friend and teacher from Southern Seminary, Donald Winters, and he called and told him about Josephine. Dr. Winters called and invited her to come to Carey, and she did.

Upon arriving in Hattiesburg in January 1958, she saw her first cross burning in someone's yard and asked, "What am I doing here?" The next day, she met Dr. Winters, and he introduced her to the faculty. Josephine met Sarah Gray who invited her to Main Street Baptist Church. They became good friends, and Josephine found her home. After she graduated from Carey, Dr. Winters called Josephine into his office and told her that he wanted her to come back to Carey and teach. She attended Southwestern Baptist Theological Seminary to earn a master's degree in music education. After graduating from Southwestern, Josephine served at several churches in the Fort Worth area as soloist and sang in the Baptist Hour choir. In 1964, First Baptist Church of Forest City, North Carolina, called her as its Minister of Music. She led in worship and was the only director of eight choirs. In 1965, Josephine returned to William Carey and remained in various capacities for the remainder of her active career.

She entered her students in Mississippi Music Teachers Association and Music Teacher National Association competitions, and they were winning first place. Josephine was a soloist for the New Orleans Philharmonic, the Mobile Symphony, and the Jackson Symphony. She also performed for the Church Music Conference of the Southern Baptist Convention. In 1990, she was awarded the Donald Winters Endowed Chair of Music. She retired from Carey in May of 2009. In September of that year, her 200 current and former students came together and presented "A Grand Night of Singing" in her honor and raised money for the Josephine D'Arpa Endowed Scholarship. Josephine is one of many students that the Winterses nurtured and supported throughout their career.

# Appendix II
# Bennett Britt

This account is based on information accumulated over a period of more than 60 years. As bit by bit was acquired, it has been stored in the repository of my memories. I do not remember all of the sources. Some of the details may be in error, but I believe the tenor to be true to the legend that has evolved over the years. Many of the anecdotes were actually told me by one or both of the Winters, themselves. I find it surprising that I have collected so much, considering the fact that the Winters rarely revealed personal information. Indeed, they might find it somewhat embarrassing for so much to be known about them. I considered Donald Winters (2 December 1910 - 20 July 1989) and Frances Weaver Winters (6 July 1908 - 29 September 1993) to have been one set of my three mentors. These two people were admired, respected, revered, and indeed, LOVED by every person who ever studied with them, I firmly believe.

When I arrived at William Carey College, Hattiesburg, Mississippi, in 1961, Dr. Winters was head of the Division of Fine Arts, under which music fell, when I was a student. He remained head when music became a department, and as the situation expanded into a School of Music with a significant growth in the number of music majors, the addition of a music therapy degree, and graduate degrees in church music and music education, he became Dean. He taught me organ, service playing, which included reading figured bass, beginning and advanced conducting, church music literature, second semester (experiential aspect) of vocal pedagogy. He conducted the Chorale (the elite choral group of the school). Mrs. Winters taught me all of my church music courses: hymnology, worship, music in worship, church music administration, all of the graded choir methods courses. She was organized and meticulous about everything she did, and always conducted herself in a professional fashion. She taught me the first semester (didactic aspect) of vocal pedagogy. I think it was in vocal pedagogy and Chorale that I came to grasp the concepts of line, tone, the practice of informed listening, etc. In other words, it was in those settings that I gained exposure to so many aspects that contribute to the development of one's musicianship.

Donald Winters grew up in Ohio and was raised in the Christian Church. I am not sure just how involved he was in the church. He was playing in dance bands, when he began attending a church in Ohio that had a true music ministry led by one of John Finley Williamson's protégés. He told me once that he was so enthralled with what he had experienced going on there, that he then knew what he wanted to do with the rest of his life. That was when he decided to attend Westminster Choir College. Dr. Winters earned bachelor and master degrees in organ performance studying with Carl Weinrich. He told me once that at some point there, he realized he also needed knowledge of the voice, and decided to do a major in voice as well with Williamson, which he did. Frances Weaver Winters was born in Greely, CO and raised in the American Baptist Church. She had completed a bachelor's degree at Denison University, and was doing graduate study in social work at Case Western Reserve University when she decided to go into music and chose Westminster Choir College. It was at Westminster Choir College that Donald and Frances Weaver met in the 1930s. In 1977, William Carey College bestowed on Mrs. Winters a much deserved honorary doctor of humane letters (LHD) degree.

In vocal pedagogy, Mrs. Winters explained to us that she was in the process of writing a vocal pedagogy text, which she later completed with her son, Donald Eugene Winters, who was a classmate of mine at William Carey. He later completed his doctorate in voice at Florida State, and returned to teach at Carey until his retirement in 2011. Mrs. Winters transmitted to us Williamson's seven principles of singing, which he began developing when he was studying with Herbert Witherspoon (see Witherspoon's little book, *Singing*). According to Mrs. Winters, Williamson did not want students taking notes, but instead maintaining continual eye contact. She explained that she was able to do this, because knowing shorthand she developed a way to surreptitiously take notes in shorthand, while maintaining continual eye contact with him. Immediately after class she would transcribe the shorthand. In time, she added an eighth principle having to do with phrasing.

I once heard her say that when she and Dr. Winters were courting, they made two very firm decisions: 1) they would never work in a Baptist Church and 2) they would never work in the South. Their first position after finishing Westminster Choir College (1941) was First Baptist Church, Atlanta. They replaced a paid quartet, receiving the same salary that had been paid the quartet. They began the first graded choir program in the state of Georgia, and one of the first, if not the first in the South. Dr. Winters told me once that the pastor, Dr. Ellis A. Fuller, was a very wise man, that he never once approached them about joining the church, or in Dr. Winters' case, becoming a Baptist. About a year after serving FBC, Dr. Winters did join FBC.

In 1943, Dr. Fuller, who had become president of Southern Baptist Theological Seminary, Louisville, KY, summoned the Winters to found a School of Church Music at the Louisville seminary. While Dr. Winters went off to the U.S. Army to serve in WWII, Mrs. Winters, now pregnant with Gene, went to Louisville, where she began developing a curriculum, based largely on the model of Westminster Choir College, and welcoming a beginning class of church musicians. Thus, they moved into education, and on Dr. Winters' return after the war, settled into a very happy situation training Southern Baptist ministers of music, with the mission of developing a standard of excellence in music in the Southern Baptist Convention. With the complete support of Dr. Fuller, he was able to choose Aeolian Skinner to build an organ of 100+ ranks, for which he told me he wrote the specification. 1950 was Dr. Fuller's last year as president, coinciding with the beginning of the Winterses' growing discontent with their situation at the seminary.

In January 1962, I received my grades for the first semester at WCU. Among them was a "C" in voice. Having been very conscientious about practicing, memorizing my pieces, and having what I thought was a good jury, etc., I expected a much higher grade. Knowing what I know now, and being very clear about what I want to hear, I think the "C" grade was very generous, but at the time, I was indignant at receiving a "C." I went to talk to my voice teacher. Fortunately, there was no answer when I knocked on his door. I then went to Dr. Winters' office a couple of doors down where I was invited in. I laid before him my grievance. Can anyone imagine such audacity?! For the next hour and a half, instead of dismissing me for my, perhaps disdainful, insubordinate, but certainly inappropriate behavior, he chose to have a very personal conversation with me. It was the only time that such a conversation between us ever happened while I was a student. As for voice, he decided that he now had a solution for my situation. He told me that I would not take voice in the semester about to start. Instead, he told me that he now had the consummate piano teacher in John Sinclair (doctorate in piano performance from Indiana U), with whom he wanted his organ students to do some study, and that instead of taking voice; I would begin piano study with Dr. Sinclair. In a most uncharacteristic manner, he began revealing some of his own story about the birth of his daughter, Janet Carol, in 1951, and of her death about nine months later, also coinciding with the onset of his difficulties at the seminary during one of SBC's periodic purges. The death of that child seemed devastating, compounded by the ending of his position at the seminary. He began the pursuit of his doctorate at Indiana U, studying organ with Oswald Ragatz. While they were at Indiana U, Mrs. Winters served as Undergraduate Coordinator-Advisor to the Dean of the School of Music there. I got the impression that Dr. Winters always had a great deal of respect and regard for Ragatz both as an artist and as a human being. (To digress for a moment, the American Guild of Organists South Mississippi Chapter usually brought a prominent organist to Hattiesburg every year for a recital on one of the major organs in the city. In 1960, it was Carl Weinrich, in 1961, Marilyn Mason, in 1962, Oswald Ragatz.) Dr. Winters completed everything but the dissertation, which was rewritten or revised several times, but never accepted. He was eventually awarded an honorary doctorate by Blue Mountain College. On two or three occasions, I heard Mrs.

Winters express bitterness toward the person blocking the acceptance of his dissertation, but I never heard Dr. Winters offer any comment about the situation, until nearing graduation, I told him that a faculty member from Cincinnati Conservatory with Meridian connections had contacted me about doing graduate study at Cincinnati, he cautioned me that the person at Indiana U that had given him so much trouble had since been placed in charge at Cincinnati. I did not pursue the Cincinnati idea any further.

In 1956, several major changes took place at William Carey College in Hattiesburg, MS. At the end of the first semester that year, the head of the Division of Fine Arts got angry for some reason, resigned his position and went across town to join the faculty of Mississippi Southern College (now University of Southern Mississippi), taking every music major with him. A young, 32-year-old theology professor, J. Ralph Noonkester, became president of Carey. At the time the school was virtually bankrupt and hanging on by a thread. While working towards the ThD degree at the seminary in Louisville, Dr. Noonkester had sung in one of Dr. Winters' ensembles. One of Dr. Noonkester's first acts was to hire Donald Winters to become head of the Division of Fine Arts at William Carey. Together with Frances Winters, they would design a "new" church music curriculum, based largely on the Westminster and Louisville seminary models, and begin developing a professional choral ensemble, the Carey College Chorale).

By the time I arrived at Carey in 1961, the Chorale had already gained a measure of prominence through its tours in the Southeast and a few states beyond. During my three years in the Chorale, we always performed everything from memory. Dr. Winters always did a Bach motet a cappella every year, except one when instead we sang Randall Thompson's *The Peaceable Kingdom.* The annual tours (12 to 14 days) consisted of something like a Baptist choral evensong (meaning there were no Anglican chant or canticles; while there was no prescribed order of service, the order was consistent with the natural sequence of worship). In addition to the Bach Motet, the literature consisted of choral pieces by such composers as Palestrina, Schutz, Rachmaninov, Brahmns, Mendelssohn, Hanson, Negro spirituals, the Russians (e.g. Tshesnokov), contemporary church music composers, etc., always closing with the Lutkin *The Lord Bless You and Keep You.* These worship services, incorporating the choral literature that had been prepared, always written by Mrs. Winters, were profoundly meaningful events.   Often the "worship service" would be followed by lighter fare in a fellowship hall or more casual setting.

In 1963 John Finley Williamson came to Carey for a week, arriving on Monday evening, 17 February. We were all assembled in the auditorium, awaiting his arrival. Dr. Winters had gone to pick him up at the Hattiesburg/ Laurel Airport. Together with Mrs. Williamson, they finally entered the auditorium about 30 minutes late. Dr. Winters had much difficulty maintaining his composure as he introduced Williamson.

Williamson began immediately by conducting Isaac Watts' great hymn, "When I survey the wondrous cross," to the *Hamburg* tune. Dr. Winters, who served as Williamson's accompanist for the week, began the hymn accompaniment four or five times before he could play the first measure correctly. I was stunned. I had never witnessed him to be so utterly rattled. (I once heard him accompany (sightread) a faculty voice recital at the very last minute, because the scheduled accompanist became unable to play, and no one else would volunteer for the task.) However, he then settled down, and there were no further problems. Very quickly, we got a foretaste of what was ahead. Williamson insisted that the first stanza was so profoundly contemplative that the meaning could only be conveyed if sung *pp.* Evidently we didn't believe him, for it took numerous starts before he was satisfied with our *pp.* There was no power struggle. He simply demonstrated that he was not going to second base before we had reached first base properly. The dynamic level then could be raised to *p* in the second stanza, he said, but for stanza three, *ppp,* if possible, then as full of gratitude as possible in the final stanza. What an experience. He had established his authority without any doubt. He repeated the performance the following morning when he directed the same hymn for the full college chapel service, receiving a similar response from the chapel assembly that he had gotten the previous evening.

From Tuesday through Friday, Dr. Williamson conducted seminars in hymnology, vocal pedagogy, choral conducting, graded choirs, music in worship, from about 8:00 a.m. until about 3:30 p.m. A choral rehearsal was held every evening for approximately two hours. He kept a tuning fork with him at all times. He relied on that to give him a pitch whenever one was needed. During both, the seminars and rehearsal, he would make what seemed the most outrageous, absolute statements, insisting that anyone disagreeing or not fully understanding, challenge him. We were all petrified, inert at first, but he would not let go of us until we began to participate. As I recall, he always backed up his statements with logical explanations, based on a long career of experience.

Throughout the week Williamson, who was 76 years old at the time of his visit, regaled us with tales and anecdotes from his long career. One of the stories was of the first meeting of Arturo Toscanini and the Westminster Choir for a rehearsal in preparation for the performance of a major choral work. Because his experience with choral ensembles had been dismal, Toscanini insisted on having several hours rehearsal time with just the chorus before a performance. However, after spending about 15 minutes with Williamson's group, he pronounced them prepared and never again scheduled another lengthy rehearsal with a Williamson directed group. (The Winterses were members of the Westminster Choir when it performed with Toscanini and Bruno Walter among other leading conductors of that day.)

I remember the Winterses telling of how Williamson would often have the choir at the track early in the morning for a mile run which he led.

Williamson also used some stunts to demonstrate various points. For instance, once, from one corner of the stage, behind the drawn curtain, with the choir in the rear at the opposite end of the auditorium, we could only see his finger conducting us.

During that week, Williamson stated his belief and prediction that if the tradition of choral music were to survive, it would be done because of church musicians developing graded choirs. Choral music was already beginning to disappear from the public school curriculum as school administrative positions were being filled more and more by people with physical education background. (Shortly after that statement was made, the demand for church musicians seemed to lessen as churches began to hire fewer and fewer full time, trained church musicians, while hiring school music teachers, including band directors, as part time employees. Consequently, church music began to disappear from the curriculum in many colleges and universities.)

The week culminated with a celebratory Choral Worship Service on Sunday afternoon, 23 February, with Dr. Williamson conducting, and Dr. Winters presiding at the console.

As the week drew to a close, Dr. Williamson mentioned that when he left Hattiesburg, he and Mrs. Williamson would be going on to Houston to visit his dear friend, Sir John Barbirolli.

Those who were present that week are unlikely to ever forget it.

There were three choral groups at Carey during my student days – 1) the Chorale, 2) the Chapel Choir – composed of music majors who were not selected for the Chorale and non-music majors who passed an audition, and 3) the Oratorio Choir, conducted by Dr. Winters – composed of all music majors, which included me, plus anyone else who wished to be a member. Shortly after first arriving at Carey, I learned that the Oratorio Choir was to perform Mendelssohn's *Hymn of Praise*. As Mendelssohn was my favorite composer at the time, I felt like I was in heaven.

I also joined First Baptist Church, Hattiesburg, where Dr. Winters was minister of music and conductor of the Adult and Youth Choirs. I soon found myself a member of the Adult and Youth Choirs, organist for the Youth Orchestra, and assistant with the Junior Boys Choir. On

Wednesdays, there were a host of activities before and after an evening meal that almost every member attended. Mrs. Winters often wrote the Wednesday evening Prayer Meeting services. Whenever she did so, the service was serene and handled with exquisite taste. Anyone not having a specific Wednesday evening activity to attend was free to attend a Bible Study led by the pastor, Dr. Clyde Bryan. Dr. Bryan, who tended to be an aesthete, was an extremely nervous man, but a man of enormous talents and a wide variety of interests. His sermons seldom were more than 5 or 6 minutes in length. Dr. Winters introduced the singing by the congregation of the Gloria Patri (Second Setting from Henry W. Greatorex' *Collection, 1851*) in the Sunday Morning Services, a rare practice in Baptist Churches, even though it was in the *Baptist Hymnal* (1956). The Adult Choir, which filled the choir loft on Sunday mornings, sang two anthems every week. The Youth Choir occupied the choir loft on Sunday evenings, and also sang two anthems every week. One Lenten season, they sang Stainer's *The Crucifixion*. Soloists were always chosen from members of the choir. In 1952, Dr. Bryan was instrumental in choosing the colonial design for the new church building. He took the building committee to New England to study many of the old churches there in minute detail. They successfully applied what they learned in carrying out their building committee responsibilities. Dr. Bryan told me that he chose the Kilgen Organ Company to build the organ (completed

1953) because the man he wanted to build the organ was an employee of Kilgen. Dr. Bryan also told me that he, himself, wrote the specification for the organ of 30 something ranks. I always thought that organ was a fine instrument. It was the organ on which I gave my senior recital. It was also the instrument on which Oswald Ragatz played the recital for AGO. A few years after I graduated, I heard that Dr. Bryan's health issues forced him to take medical leave. He eventually began his own tour agency, and led many tours of Europe. Looking back, it now occurs to me that every single worship service I attended there was a truly edifying experience, unique in my experience.

Mrs. Winters retired in 1973. However, she continued to write the worship service for the annual tours. She was also the driving force behind the successful acquisition of the personal library of Clarence Dickinson through arrangements made with Dickinson's widow with the great support of Dickinson's assistant, George Litch Knight. Dickinson founded the School of Sacred Music at Union Theological Seminary. He was also a founding member of the American Guild of Organists. This collection, housed in the Smith-Rouse Library on the campus of William Carey, is one of only a few of its kind.

During the last years of his career at Carey, Dr. Winters included First United Methodist Church, Thibodaux, LA (where I was organist/choirmaster) on the annual Chorale tour three times (1977, 1979, and 1981, his last one). He also served as my organ consultant when I embarked on a campaign that resulted in the Wicks Organ Company, Highland, IL producing a custom-built 2-manual pipe organ for First United Methodist Church. I believe that any builder would have been proud to claim that instrument. Dr. Winters played the first service on that organ Easter Sunday, 1983. After I left that church, the organ gradually fell into disuse, and is rarely used today. Instead, a "praise" band has taken its place.

Dr. Winters was diagnosed with stage four cancer shortly after completion of this project. It was in remission in 1986 when Dr. John Sinclair returned to Carey to present a recital. I was invited to attend a small gathering at the Winters' home afterward. As we sat together talking, we all remembered the Marilyn Mason recital (Incidentally, Dr. Robert Gauldin had written a review of that recital for the Hattiesburg American) and that given by Ragatz as well. Dr. Winters mentioned that he thought the Kilgen was in need of a new console. A short while later, I learned that the Kilgen was being rebuilt and expanded to 4-manuals and 59 ranks by the Reuter Organ Company. During that evening, in response to my request, Dr. Winters also agreed to return to FUMC, Thibodaux for a weekend choral workshop with my choir, ending with the choir, conducted by him and with me at the console, in a Choral Worship Service that included nine anthems. It occurred Sunday, 15 March 1987, and was a glorious occasion. Mrs. Winters paid me a great compliment when she told me after the service that they (FUMC) had no idea what they had in me. Mrs. Winters had come with him – she later told me to assist him medically, that the cancer had returned with a vengeance, and it was against everyone's advice that he came. Mrs. Winters told me that he had insisted on coming, however, because he had "promised Bennett." Shortly after that event, his condition worsened, and when I attended a rare Chorale Alumni Reunion in July of that year, he was paralyzed and in a wheel chair. Yet, from that wheelchair, he conducted the Alumni Chorale in a Choral Worship Service that Sunday in First Baptist Church, Hattiesburg.

It was at this time that Dr. Winters asked me to play one of the dedicatory recitals (the last of the series) on the now newly rebuilt Reuter Organ. This I did on Sunday, 15 October 1989. Mrs. Winters hosted a reception for me in their home.

Sadly, Dr. Winters had died in late July. There were many alumni who returned for his memorial service, becoming another large Alumni Chorale to once again sing some of the literature he had taught us, with voices that seemed to me to still produce that dazzling, rich, brilliant, virile tone, only with more maturity now.

Mrs. Winters died 29 September 1993, following hip replacement surgery, as she was preparing to return for the 50th Anniversary Celebration of the founding of the Southern Baptist Theological Seminary School of

Church Music. Again, a large Alumni Chorale assembled to participate in her memorial service. Her son, Dr. Gene Winters decided that given Mrs. Winters' love of hymnology and longstanding ties to the Hymn Society, it would be most appropriate that hymns be the focus of the service.

The following are some examples of the many sayings of the Winters.

I heard Mrs. Winters express the following principle numerous times: "It is not so important that one knows what one doesn't want to hear and then attempts to get rid of it. It is important that one knows what one wants to hear, and how to build it." I wonder if we all, indeed our current society included, might not be wise to adhere to that principle more often.

While leaving class one day, Mrs. Winters overheard a debate about the application of certain techniques when administering the church music program. She stepped in and reminded us all, "Remember, we are presenting a Person, not a program."

Mrs. Winters maintained that choral conductors should listen to the Budapest Quartet (modified later to" a good string quartet") and strive to have their choral ensembles execute attacks, releases, etc. in similar fashion.

On numerous occasions, I heard Dr. Winters state firmly his opinion that "An organ stands or falls on the voicing of the pipes," a process to which he thought that Aeolian Skinner gave great care.

Dr. Winters once shared with me a very revealing observation from his experience that had served to shape his approach to music making. He said he gradually became aware that often as a choral performance began, he would find himself thinking, "That's very nicely done, good tone, diction, proper balance, etc." The second piece would follow. "That's very nice, too." As the third and fourth pieces followed, he realized his interest was waning, and he was becoming tired and bored. He resolved from the time of that realization, that even though his performance might be flawed, he was determined that it would never be boring!

12 July 2021

# Appendix III

## *The Ministry Of Music*

THE WESTMINSTER PLAN for the ministry of music in the Church is not a new idea, even though it has often been characterized as such. It encourages the restoration to the church of that program which belonged to the church years ago, namely, the inclusion of the whole membership in worship. It fulfills the Psalmist's command, "Let the people praise Thee, O God, let *all* the people praise Thee." Briefly, the objective of this plan is that of interesting, as far as is humanly possible, the children, young people, and adults of the congregation in a closer working relationship with their Church through the ministry of music. It is not a program designed to help the Church for just today nor for just this year. It is a comprehensive educational program which, year in and year out, has in preparation both today's services and tomorrow's choir.

THE CHANCEL CHOIR is open to singers of good Christian character who are High School graduates or beyond high school age. Auditions are required. To this choir falls the responsibility of leadership. It furnishes the music for the regular Sunday services, leads the congregational singing and is a constant example both to Youth Choirs and congregation in its attitude of worship.

THE YOUTH CHOIR SCHOOL is established for the purpose of training the Singing Youth of Today for the Singing Church of Tomorrow. This is possible not only through offering training to the youth of our Sunday School and Training Union in the traditions and practice of choir singing, but also through offering them actual service in the church. It is a part of the educational program of the Church in which religious music is used as an educational factor and provides a service outlet along with its special instruction.

## THE YOUTH CHOIRS

*The Cherub Choir*
  (children 4 to 6)
*The Canto Choir*
  (children 6, 7, and 8)
*The Carol Choir*
  (girls 9, 10, 11)
*The Crusader's Choir*
  (boys 9, 10, 11)

*The Celestial Choir*
  (girls 12, 13, 14)
*The Challenger Choir*
  (boys 12, 13, 14)
*The Chapel Choir*
  (Senior High School boys
  and girls)
  Auditions required.

## THE ATLANTA YOUTH

REV. J. E. RUSSELL, Pastor of Rock Springs Presbyterian Church, who will deliver the Christmas message at the Sunrise Service.

MR. DONALD WINTERS

# CHRISTMAS SUNRISE SERVICE
### DECEMBER 25, 1941
### 8 to 9 A. M.
## FIRST BAPTIST CHURCH

Presiding—Miss Alverta Sedgwick, Chairman
Young People's Commission.

Music—Chapel and Chancel Choirs, First Baptist Church
Mr. Donald Winters, Director

Announcements ............ Miss Sedgwick
Hymn—"O Come All Ye Faithful"
—Congregation
Carol "Carol of the Bells—Ukrainian
Carol—Chapel and Chancel Choirs.
Prayer—Rev. E. R. Carter, Pastor, West
End Christian Church.
Hymn—"The First Noel"—
Congregation
Christmas Scripture—Luke 2: 1-20—
Rev. Luther W. McArthur, Pastor
Avondale Estates Methodist
Church.

Hymn—"O Little Town of Bethlehem—
Congregation
Carol—"Joseph Came Seeking a Rest-
ing Place"—Ernest Willoughby.
Chapel and Chancel Choirs.
The Christmas Message—Rev. J. E.
Russell, Pastor, Rock Springs Pres-
byterian Church.
Prayer—Dr. Ryland Knight, Pastor,
Second Ponce de Leon Baptist
Church.
Hymn—"Joy to the World"—
Congregation
Benediction—Dr. Knight.

The Chapel Choir (High School),
First Baptist Church, Atlanta,
December, 1941.

## Seminary Choir Renders Skillfull Musical Program

The service in song presented Saturday night in the Farmville Baptist Church by The Southern Baptist Church was an inspirational musical event, heard by an audience that filled the church auditorium.

A splendidly trained choir, capably directed by Donald Winters, rendered a difficult program of church music of the highest order. The choir numbered splendid solo voices, which carried the solo parts to a technical finish.

With equal facility the men and women of the School of Church Music of the Southern Baptist Theological Seminary moved from modulated passages to great crescendos, filling the church auditorium.

Interposed between anthems, hymns and great church music, members of the choir recited passages of scripture and messages of a living faith. There were also interludes of organ music, skillfuly played by Kenneth Pool, organist of the School of Church Music.

The final number, for which the audience stood, was Handel's Hallelujah Chorus from "The Messiah." After the choral benediction, the choir returned to the platform to render a delightfully skilled, short program of Negro spirituals.

Farmville, Va.
1950

THE GREENVILLE PIEDMONT,
GREENVILLE, SOUTH CAROLINA
WEDNESDAY, FEBRUARY 14, 1951

## Southern Seminary Choir Gives Dignity To Music

By ELEANOR BARTON

In tribute to Dr. Ellis Adams Fuller, late president of the Southern Baptist Theological Seminary in Louisville, Ky., the Southern Seminary Choir has this season dedicated a program worthy of the great minister, the beloved man, and the administrative genius under whose leadership the School of Church Music was founded, have sung more than 20 times on a tour through five states.

Under the direction of Donald Withers, with Kenneth Pool at the organ, the choir of approximately 40 voices was presented in concert here last night before an audience that filled to capacity the auditorium of Pendleton Street Baptist Church. The choir is near the end of its tour which has provided a fatiguing if not gruelling schedule.

If the program which they presented in Greenville last night is a sample of the type of church music to which the Louisville school aspires, a new and superior conception of the role of music in the worship service has been inspired. It augers well for the future of church music, for the dignity of its place in religion, for the beauty which it brings to daily living, and for the faith which it expresses in God and man.

The program proper began with an oratorio, in miniature by Johannes Brahms, a setting of Psalm II (OP, 29, No. 2) in which the choir sang a capella. It is a monumental work in three parts which would discourage an experienced choir that had the full support of an organ accompaniment, and yet some felt that the Seminary Choir did perhaps its outstanding work in this number, without accompaniment of any kind.

It ended with Handel's "Hallelujah Chorus" from "The Messiah." And if the volume was less than this matchless work demands, the fine spirit with which it was sung offered some compensation.

The program included "Truth, Crushed to Earth, Shall Rise Again" by Claude M. Almand of Louisville, who was married later last summer to the former Miss Lenoir Patton of Greenville.

Other numbers had been chosen to illustrate many of the radio messages and chapel talks by the late President Fuller, excerpts from which were given by members of the choir. If their content seemed sometimes based upon the social sciences and principles of political economy rather than upon the Scriptures, it was understandable in view of the purpose which in large measure determined their choice.

On other occasions the music is doubtless allowed to speak for itself, and the Scriptural references upon which they are based to form the only proper norm.

The program last night included a group of spirituals which were adeptly sung.

Mr. Pool, of Greenville, and an alumnus of Furman University is unquestionably one of America's finest young musicians and an organist of marked ability.

## Baptist Choir, Touring South, Is Heard Here

BY E. CLYDE WHITLOCK.

In the course of a tour of Southern States the choir of the School of Church Music of Southern Baptist Theological Seminary, Louisville, was heard in a service of choral music Wednesday night at Broadway Baptist Church by a sobered congregation. The singers remembered in their devotions the plight of Fort Worth.

The well balanced choir of 42 mixed voices devoted themselves to a program which leaned toward the modern, especially the fine unaccompanied music of the old Russian church, but not touching the pre-Bach era. The Damrosch setting of the exalting Luther chorale, "A Mighty Fortress," made a stirring beginning, followed immediately by a strangely orthodox offering from Roy Harris; then a modified creed by Carl Mueller and three Russian items, including the inspiring "Cherubim Song" of Tschaikowsky.

American Composers Randall Thompson, Dickinson and Dawson were represented, then the German classics in "A Saving Health" by Brahms, perhaps the best sung item of the program, a Bach chorale and Schubert's exultant "The Omnipotence."

An extra group of Negro spirituals was added, including "Peter, Ring Dem Bells," "Steal Away" and "Ezekiel Saw the Wheel."

Between numbers throughout the program members of the choir gave appropriate scripture quotations and prayers.

The group, after a slight initial nervousness in attacks, exhibited fullbodied, resonant tone, admirable adherence to pitch, alert response to direction and exceptional distinctness of text. Donald Winters, director, invoked the best traditions of a cappella choral singing.

Kenneth Pool, organist, played a preliminary program from Marcello, Kuhnau, Scheidt and Bach with considerable digital skill, and during the program the "Adagio" from the Bach "Toccata in C Major" with such an excess of speed and deficiency of imagination as to render it stolidy perfunctory.

Broadway Baptist Church
Ft. Worth, Texas

## Music School Choir Wins Applause

Dear Dr. McCall:

"Last fall I had a letter from you telling me about the proposed tour of the Choir of the School of Church Music of the Louisville Seminary, and of the possibility of presenting this choir in our church.

"I want you to know that this choir gave a splendid performance from the point of view of all of the musicians who heard the concert. What was even more important was that this concert was given in the form of a most reverent worship service; which was deeply appreciated by everyone present. Mr. Pool added to the program in no small measure with his masterful playing of the organ. High praise has been given for the type music used by this group. Raymond Anderson, head of the Department of Music at Birmingham

Southern College was loud in his praise of the type program presented, as well as the high calibre musicianship displayed in the performance.

"I want to thank you for telling me about the tour, and I also want to thank Messrs. Winters and Pool and the Seminary Choir for what they are doing to advance the cause of better church music throughout our denomination." —Frank A. Heberlin, Minister of Music, First Baptist Church, Birmingham, Ala.

* * *

"Just a line to tell you how much our people enjoyed the choir from the Louisville Seminary last Friday night. This is the second time the choir has been to our church for a religious concert and our people could not say enough nice things about them. . . . Without a doubt it is the finest choir of its kind I have

ever heard. I can think of no finer advertising for the Seminary than these 38 singers, who with deep consecration and beautiful music, are singing the gospel story and representing our great Seminary. . . . I would like to thank the Seminary for making it possible for the choir to make this tour and hope that before too long they can come back and be with us in our church."—John E. Barnes, Jr., Pastor Main Street Baptist Church, Hattiesburg, Miss.

* * *

"The Seminary Choir came to our church a couple of weeks ago to give us an evening of inspiring music and song. They did just that in a very acceptable manner. . . . Many of the musicians, choir directors, and choir members of our city were present. Everybody

(Continued on Page 8)

### CHOIR APPLAUSE
(Continued from Page 3)

agreed that it was one of the best musical programs But we have ever had in our church. They really did a good job of reminding us of the place of our Seminary in the life of our denomination. The choir is a credit to the Seminary. . . . Mr. Winters and Mr. Pool acquitted themselves in a marvelous way."—John L. Slaughter, Pastor First Baptist Church, Birmingham, Ala.

"I just wanted to drop you a word concerning the choir from the School of Church Music. The program which they gave in our church last week was definitely the best we have ever had. Their singing is superb in every way. We had a large crowd, and one of our radio stations made a recording, and broadcast it later in the evening. The work of the choir was highly commended by everyone. Kenneth Pool was very impressive with his organ numbers, which were highly appreciated. The tour of this choir is certainly a credit to the fine work being done by our Seminary. I thought you would like to know the reaction here. . . ."—W. Fred Kendall, Pastor First Baptist Church, Jackson, Tenn.

"We really enjoyed the program of music which the choir of the School of Music presented to us a week ago Sunday. Our people enjoyed it to the fullest. The choir is unusually well trained and is a genuine credit to our beloved Seminary. I enjoyed having fellowship with Donald Winters and the students. They are worthy representatives of Southern Seminary."—Harold J. Purdy, Pastor Belmont Heights Baptist Church, Nashville, Tenn.

"A couple of weeks ago we had the seminary choir in our church one evening, and the service which they conducted, and the spirit of the choir members in our homes and community was such that our people were overwhelmed. In five years I have not seen the members of our church in particular, and the people of our city in general, more unanimous in their approval than they were of the choir and its work. —J. H. Kyzar, Pastor First Baptist Church, Greenwood, Miss.

MAY, 1952      THE TIE

**HATTIESBURG, MISSISSIPPI, SATURDAY, OCT. 22, 1966**

## At Carey College

# Thomas Fine Arts Center to be dedicated Sunday

BY MARJORIE ROWDEN

One of the biggest events in the history of William Carey College will take place at 3 p.m. Sunday as Thomas Fine Arts Center is formally dedicated.

Citizens of Hattiesburg have been invited to fill the 1200-seat auditorium as the $700,000 building is dedicated. Dr. Earl Kelly, president of the Mississippi Baptist Convention, will deliver the main address of the afternoon. Preceded by this will be an unveiling of an oil portrait of Mr. and Mrs. R. B. Thomas, for whom the building has been named.

The Thomases, longtime residents of Hattiesburg, have been generous benefactors of the school. Hundreds of individual students have been given the right to enjoy Christian high education because of the Thomas's interest and support.

The portrait has been painted by an artist in Neiman-Marcus of Dallas, and is a gift to the college from Mr. and Mrs. W. C. Carpenter of Brownwood, Texas. Mrs. Carpenter is the daughter of Mr. and Mrs. Thomas. Many out of town friends and relatives of the Thomases have been invited to attend the occasion.

An outstanding musical performance by an 80-voice chorus will also be heard at 3 p.m. Sunday. Dr. Benjamin Dunford, professor of music theory at Carey, has written an original cantata, "Psalm 103." It will include along with the chorus a soloist, and brass and percussion instruments. It will be majestic in scope.

The Thomas Fine Arts Center has been built by funds raised during the 1963 Carey Development Program. It includes, in addition to the 1200-seat auditorium, facilities for a complete music program. The spacious lecture halls, piano practice rooms, recital hall, and offices are modern and functional in every detail.

The gigantic stage of Thomas Fine Arts Center Auditorium is the largest in the entire area. It is capable of holding any major musical or dramatic performance adequately. The loft above was an afterthought; because of generous financial support on the part of the Jimmy Pope family of Richton and the Bass family of Lumberton, it became a reality. The loft will store elaborate staging and decorating props.

The Birmingham Symphony Orchestra will be heard on Monday night in a special dedicatory concert in the new facilities. Under the direction of Amerigo Marion the Symphony has received nation-wide acclaim.

Tickets are on sale for $2.20 each. Sponsor cards entitling two people to the Symphony are selling for $25; and patron cards also allowing two persons entrance are selling for $10. Special reserved seats will be held for these categories only.

All tickets are available at the following places: Essex House, Brothers - Matison Company, Johnson Music Store, Roseberry Piano House, Waldoff's on Pine, and the Box Office of Thomas Hall. Tickets may also be purchased by calling 583-3225, the Music Department office. The concert will begin at 8:15 Monday night.

The Four Freshman, nationally famous singing group will be presented in Thomas Fine Arts Auditorium Thursday night, Oct. 27. This event is being sponsored by the Student Government Assn. Tickets are available at the Student Affairs Office for $1 per student and $2 per adult.

The week's activities will be rounded out by the presentation on Monday evening, Oct. 31, of Miss Gianna D'Angelo, coloratura soprano of the Metropolitan Opera. Miss D'ngelo is being presented by the Community Concert Association as their first event of the season.

Completing the beautification of Thomas Fine Arts Center is a multicolored fountain now being presented to the school by Bobby Chain, local businessman, in memory of his mother, Mrs. Grace Sellers Chain. It will take the place of the old Philo Fountain, which was a traditional feature on the Carey campus that dated back to Women's College days. It was demolished in order for the Thomas Fine Arts Center to be built.

All Hattiesburg citizens are urged and invited to join the Carey student body, faculty, and staff in this unusually fine dedicatory week that has been planned.

---

Thursday, October 19, 1967 **Hattiesburg AMERICAN** Page 19

# Carey Chorale to sing with Orleans philharmonic

The Carey College Chorale which will be featured with the New Orleans Philharmonic Orchestra has a history of bringing to South Mississippi choral works which are seldom heard in the area. Their performance of G. Verdi's Te Deum, under the direction of Werner Torkanowsky on Friday night, Oct. 20 at Thomas Hall Auditorium on the William Carey College campus in Hattiesburg, will continue that tradition.

The ensemble dates from 1956 when Donald Winters came to the college as head of the division of fine arts in the newly reorganized co-educational Baptist school. Since that time the Chorale has gained a wide reputation as an ensemble equally at home in both contemporary and traditional choral forms. Through its national tours, recordings, and appearances before the Southern Baptist Convention, its place as a significant force in the establishment of musical criteria in Baptist Colleges has been assured.

In their expanded organization, the Carey Oratorio Choir, the Chorale has premiered two major contemporary choral works, Benjamin Dunford's Psalm 123 and Robert Gauldin's Herod and the Magi. From the traditional literature they have presented the rarely performed Israel in Egypt by G. F. Handel, the Brahms Requiem, Randall Thompson's The Peaceable Kingdom, and, with the Mobile Symphony Orchestra, the St. Matthew Passion by Bach.

Members of the Chorale are from cities as far distant as Zurich, Switzerland, but all are united in their efforts to restore sacred choral music to its rightful place in the concert repertory. Thirty-one of the singers hold positions as choir director, accompanist, or soloist in various churches in the area. Eighteen are preparing to teach in the public schools of their home states. A large percentage of the Chorale members begin graduate studies immediately upon completion of their work at William Carey College, and some have earned doctorates and are now teaching in colleges and universities in the South.

Academic and musical standards are high and competition is keen among the students. Chorale members report to college two weeks before the beginning of classes and often find themselves rehearsing late into the night. Donald Winters is assisted by Miss Josephine D'Arpa, a native of Tampa, and a graduate of the Southwestern Baptist Seminary in Ft. Worth, Texas, as voice coach. Mrs. Helen McWhorter, organist of the First Baptist Church of Hattiesburg and a member of the piano faculty at Carey College serves as accompanist.

The appearance of the Chorale with the New Orleans Symphony will be the first performance of the Carey singers with conductor Werner Torkanowsky. The Verdi Te Deum is a hymn of praise for orchestra, double chorus, and soprano soloist. Miss D'Arpa will be featured as soloist. The orchestra will also play the Overture to Russian and Ludmilla by Glinka, Ravel's Daphnis and Chloe Suite, No. 2, and Dvorak's New World Symphony. The concert, which will be given in the Thomas Fine Arts Center at 8:30 coincides with the annual meeting of the Mississippi Music Teachers Association being held on the Carey campus. Members of the association will be the guests of the college for the performance.

Tickets are on sale at the Thomas Hall box office, at Fine Bros.-Matison, Essex House, Johnson Music Co., Roseberry Piano House, Waldoff's and Milton's.

# Dickinson Memorial Library at Wm Carey

## Dedication On April 27 Marks Official Opening

The Clarion-Ledger JACKSON DAILY NEWS 17
Sunday, April 22, 1973                          SECTION E

The Dickinson Memorial Library of Church Music on the campus of William Carey College will be officially opened to the public on Friday morning, April 27, at 11 o'clock in a dedication service as part of a two-day conference of church musicians, educators and historians.

The Dickinson Memorial Library contains the personal manuscripts, correspondence, memorabilia of Clarence and Helen Dickinson, members of the faculty of Union Theological Seminary, New York, and two of the most significant influences of American Church Music in the twentieth century.

Clarence Dickinson served as dean of the School of Sacred Music of Union Theological Seminary and as organist-recitalist throughout the United States. For fifty years he also served as organist-choirmaster of the Brick Presbyterian Church of New York City, in which position he made many unique contributions to the community. He was a founding member of the American Guild of Organists and of the Hymn Society of America, and was editor of the 1937 edition of the Presbyterian Hymnal.

Helen Dickinson was for many years a teacher of humanities courses at Union Theological Seminary and the Me-morial Library will house her books and teaching materials. Clarence and Helen Dickinson collaborated for many years in the collection and publishing of religious folks songs of many nations.

The central collection of the library will contain over 5000 books and musical scores from the personal library of the Dickinsons and various students who have supported the establishment of this memorial at William Carey College. The major contributor from among the Dickinson students is Dr. George Litch Knight, minister of the Lafayette Avenue Presbyterian Church of Brooklyn, N.Y., whose large collection of books and paintings has been added to the library.

Dr. Donald Winters, dean of the School of Music at Carey College, observed, "The Dickinson Memorial Collection will create on the William Carey College campus a major research library for church musicians and historians. It will greatly strengthen our graduate programs in church music and the recently established undergraduate humanities programs."

The festival is being made possible through the assistance of Mississippi Arts Commission and National Endowment of the Arts; Friends of the Clarence Dickinsons; Church Music Department, Mississippi Baptist Convention Board, Hattiesburg Civic Arts Council; and South Mississippi chapter, American Guild of Organists.

The festival program begins on Thursday, April 26. Registration will begin in the lobby of Thomas Auditorium at 1:00 p.m.

All church musicians and interested persons are invited to attend.

*The School of Music*

*of*

*William Carey College*

*Hattiesburg, Mississippi*

*cordially invites you to attend a*

*Festival*

*April 26th and 27th, 1973*

*Celebrating the Dedication and Opening of the*

*Clarence Dickinson*

*Memorial Library*

*with the*

*Centenary of Dr. Dickinson's Birth*

*and*

*One Hundred Years of*

*American Church Music*

BLUE MOUNTAIN COLLEGE

CITATION

DONALD WINTERS

Donald Winters was born in Greenville, Ohio, December 2, 1910. He attended school in Greenville having graduated from the Greenville High School. He holds a diploma from Westminister Choir College, Princeton, New Jersey; the Bachelor of Music degree and Masters degree from Teachers College, Columbia University. He has completed further graduate work at Northwestern University, School of Music and Indiana University School of Music.

Mr. Winters has a distinguished record of his contributions to his chosen discipline, to Christian education, and to the Baptist denomination. He was the Co-Founder and Acting Administrative Head of the School of Church Music at the Southern Baptist Theological Seminary, 1945-1952. He has built the William Carey College School of Music to one of the most outstanding in the South in Church Music. He has strengthened the program of Christian education in Mississippi through his leadership role of Dean of the School of Music of Carey College.

His service to the Southern Baptist Convention is notable. He has served as a member of the Executive Committee, Southern Baptist Music Conference, and was elected to serve as President, 1967-69. In 1969 he was in charge of all music at the Southern Baptist Convention.

Mr. Winters is a Christian gentleman who has sought opportunities to serve his fellowman and to serve God. He has the distinction of holding a major leadership role in every Baptist church of which he has been a member. He founded the School of Choirs at First Baptist Church, Atlanta, Georgia, and has served as Music Director in churches in Kentucky, Indiana, and Hattiesburg, Mississippi where he is presently serving as Minister of Music at the First Baptist Church.

The Board of Trustees presents Mr. Donald Winters for the honorary degree of Doctor of Music: In recognition of his dedication to and his recognized accomplishments in the field of music; of his contribution to children and young people throughout the Southern Baptist Convention; in honor of his commitment to Christian education; and for lifelong integrity and loyalty to the values implicit in the spirit and history of Blue Mountain College, the trustees offer this citation.

This the thirty-first day of May, nineteen hundred seventy,

Joe Jack Hurst, President, Board of Trustees

E. Harold Fisher, President, Blue Mountain College

IN APPRECIATION...

*Donald and Frances Winters*

Mississippi Baptist Church
Music Conference
February 16, 1979

FOR YEARS OF SERVICE

| | |
|---|---|
| 1930 | Frances Weaver receives BA in Religious Education, Denison University |
| 1939 | Frances Weaver and Donald Winters receive BM degree from Westminster Choir College |
| 1940 | Donald Winters and Frances Weaver are married |
| 1941 | Donald receives MM from Westminster Choir College |
| 1941 | Donald begins service as Minister of Music while Frances serves as Assistant Minister of Music at First Baptist Church, Atlanta, Georgia |
| 1943 | Donald enters the United States Army |
| 1943-1952 | Frances serves as Professor of Church Music at Southern Baptist Theological Seminary, Louisville, Kentucky |
| 1945-1952 | Donald is Administrator and Professor of Music at Southern Baptist Theological Seminary, Louisville, Kentucky |
| 1946-1952 | Donald serves as Organist-Director at Broadway Baptist Church, Louisville, Kentucky |
| 1952-1956 | Donald attends Indiana University while Frances serves as the Assistant to the Dean of the School of Music at that university |
| 1953-1956 | Donald serves as Organist at First Baptist Church, Bloomington, Indiana |
| 1956 | Donald becomes Head of the Division of Fine Arts of William Carey College |
| 1958 | Frances joins the faculty of William Carey College as Professor of Church Music |
| 1959-1969 | Donald serves as Minister of Music of First Baptist Church, Hattiesburg, Mississippi |
| 1967-1969 | Donald serves as President of the Southern Baptist Church Music Conference |
| 1969 | Donald becomes Dean of the School of Music of William Carey College |
| 1970 | Donald receives Doctor of Music degree from Blue Mountain College, Blue Mountain, Mississippi |
| 1972 | The Frances Winters Graduate Scholarship Fund is established at William Carey College |
| 1974 | Frances retires from teaching |
| 1977 | Frances receives Doctor of Humane Letters degree from William Carey College |
| 1978 | Donald becomes President of the Mississippi Baptist Church Music Conference |
| 1978 | Frances' composition is published and premiered, Lafayette Avenue Presbyterian Church, Brooklyn, New York |
| 1978 | Frances begins work with Television Ministry of First Baptist Church, Hattiesburg |
| 1979 | Donald Winters becomes Dean Emeritus, School of Music, William Carey College |

A CONCERT

Honoring

DR. DONALD WINTERS, Dean Emeritus, *School of Music*
DR. FRANCES WINTERS, Professor Emerita, *School of Music*

by the

CAREY COLLEGE CHORALE

Buryl Red, Guest Conductor
Charles E. Endsley, Guest Accompanist

PROGRAM

| | |
|---|---|
| From A GERMAN REQUIEM . . . . . . . . . . . . . . . . . . . . . . . . . Brahms | |
| "How Lovely Is Thy Dwelling Place" | |
| I Will Arise and Go to Jesus . . . . . . . . . . . . . . . . . . . . . . . Arr. Shaw-Parker | |
| *Psalm for Today . . . . . . . . . . . . . . . . . . . . . . . . . . . . . . Buryl Red | |
| My Eternal King . . . . . . . . . . . . . . . . . . . . . . . . . . . . . Jane Marshall | |
| Alleluia . . . . . . . . . . . . . . . . . . . . . . . . . . . . . . . Randall Thompson | |
| The Lord's Prayer . . . . . . . . . . . . . . . . . . . . . . . . . . Charles E. Endsley | |
| From BEGINNINGS . . . . . . . . . . . . . . . . . . . . . . . . . . . . Buryl Red | |
| "Glorious in Holiness" | |

Assisted by:

| | |
|---|---|
| Narrator: | Roger Phillips |
| Percussion: | David Baughman |
| | Jan E. Douglas |
| Piano: | Philip Fortenberry |

CAREY'S FIVE DEANS will issue degrees, both graduate and undergraduate, on May 5 during annual commencement ceremonies at 10 A.M. Dr. Noonkester, left, chats with all five dressed in their academic gowns: Dr. Donald Winters (to retire as Dean of the School of Music in May); Dr. Steve Robinson, School of Business; Dr. Flora Blackstock, School of Nursing; Dr. Hugh Dickens, Graduate School; and Dr. Joseph Ernest, Academic Vice-president and Dean of the School of Arts and Sciences. Dr. Dickens is also Executive Vice-president of the College.

Left: Program for the Red concert, Commencement week-end, 1979, Above: At Donald's last official Commencement at Carey, he is pictured with other degree-awarding Deans, May 5, 1979. From The Profile, Spring, 1979, p. 7.

# The Southern Baptist Theological Seminary

2825 LEXINGTON ROAD • LOUISVILLE, KENTUCKY 40280

December 4, 1984

Dr. and Mrs. Donald Winters
School of Music
William Carey College
Hattiesburg, Mississippi    39401

Dear Don and Frances:

On behalf of the entire faculty and staff of the School of Church
Music at Southern Seminary, I am writing to convey congratulations
on the occasion of the naming of the School of Music at William
Carey College for you.  This is certainly an appropriate recognition
of the investment which the two of you have made in the lives of
hundreds of young musicians as a contribution to their musical and
ministerial development.

Your contributions to the development of a program of instruction
at this institution  are also recognized and appreciated.  I have
asked Hugh McElrath to undertake the writing of a history of the
School of Church Music at Southern Seminary, and in this document
the role which you had in establishing a solid foundation for the
program of church music instruction currently taking place here will
be given thorough coverage.

Continuing best wishes to you.

Sincerely,

Milburn Price, Dean
School of Church Music

MP/df

# New Orleans Baptist Theological Seminary

3939 Gentilly Boulevard • New Orleans, Louisiana 70126-4858 • (504) 282-4455

Division of
Church Music Ministries

December 6, 1984


Drs. Donald and Frances Winters
200 Patton Avenue
Hattiesburg, Mississippi    39401

Dear Frances and Don,

Thank you for your gracious hospitality to me Tuesday evening.  It
was certainly a wonderful evening and I believe it was a very appropriate and wise move on the part of the Carey College administration
to name to School of Music in your honor.  You have been a blessing
to the lives of numerous students as well as colleagues like myself
in various other institutions.  Thank you for what you have meant to
me personally.  May the Lord bless you now and in the days to come.

Frances, I have recommended that our Music Library purchase your and
Gene's new book on Vocal Pedagogy.  I have also sent the brochure to
Mr. Steve Skinner, our new voice teacher who will be arriving on cam-
us fresh from Indiana University in January.  Congratulations to you
and Gene on this very impressive text.

Blessings on you in this beautiful time of Advent and Christmas.

Sincerely,

Harry Eskew, Professor
Music History and Hymnology

/dr

Mention church or choral music to anyone who has been associated with William Carey College or has been involved in music with the Mississippi and Southern Baptist conventions for very long and they will likely think of Donald and Frances Winters.

Their more than 20 years of contributions to music at William Carey College and among Southern Baptist church music circles have made them a legacy.

Carey trustees, in recognition of the couple's contributions, and to immortalize the Winters legacy, approved last September the naming of the College's School of Music in their honor.

This evening's events are a celebration of the naming of the Donald and Frances Winters School of Music at William Carey College.

From the music department's humble beginnings in 1956, Donald and Frances Winters guided the program to national recognition, to school status and established Carey's first graduate-level degree program — the master's in music. Along the way, the School attained recognition for its strong and innovative church and choral music programs.

Prior to coming to Carey, Dr. Winters served as acting administrative dean of the School of Church Music at Southern Baptist Theological Seminary in Louisville, Ky. Dr. Winters, along with Mrs. Winters, founded the School of Church Music and was conductor of the seminary's choir, whose annual tours covered more than 100 cities in the South.

He has served as minister of music at Broadway Baptist Church, Louisville, Ky.; First Baptist Church, Bloomington, Ind.; Main Street and First Baptist churches, Hattiesburg; and First Baptist Church, Atlanta.

In 1940, while at First Baptist Church, Atlanta, Dr. and Mrs. Winters established the School of Choirs, which has become known as the graded choir program and is now used in churches across the Southern Baptist Convention.

A graduate of Westminster Choir College in Princeton, N.J., (B.M., M.M.) Dr. Winters completed residence requirements for his doctorate in music from Indiana University. Mrs. Winters is a graduate of Denison University and the Westminster Choir College and has done additional graduate studies at Columbia University, Western Reserve University and the University of Louisville. Prior to joining the Carey faculty she served as assistant to the dean of the Indiana University School of Music.

Dr. Winters received the honorary doctor of music degree from Blue Mountain College in 1970 and Mrs. Winters received the doctor of humane letters degree from William Carey in 1977.

Mrs. Winters and son Gene, assistant professor of music at Carey, recently completed work on a book, "Vocal Pedagogy: A Guide to Singing Skills."

The Winters' other son, John, owns several restaurants in the Denver, Colo. area.

Since Donald and Frances Winters are responsible for bringing Carey's School of Music the national recognition in church and choral music it has received, it only seems natural that the School be named in their honor. In so doing, Carey recommits itself to carrying on the rich tradition of church and choral music that the Winters made legendary in Mississippi and throughout the Southern Baptist Convention.

*The William Carey College Chorale and Chorale Alumni*
of
*The Winters School of Music*
**WILLIAM CAREY COLLEGE**
Hattiesburg, Mississippi

present

# HANDEL'S THE MESSIAH

SOLOISTS
THERESA McBEE, Soprano, '84
BEVERLY TRAMES, Alto, '79
TERRY BOWERS, Tenor, '88
SIDNEY BUCKLEY, Bass, '91
CHARLES ENSLEY, Organist, '90
JEFF MULLAND, Harpsichordist

DECEMBER 4, 1984
EIGHT O'CLOCK
Smith Auditorium
Thomas Fine Arts Center

# Carey music school gets new name as couple recognized

Musicians from across the nation joined William Carey College Tuesday night in honoring Dr. and Mrs. Donald Winters, founders of the college's school of music, for their more than 20 years of "unprecedented devotion" to the school.

Carey trustees approved last September the naming of the school of music in honor of the couple, who came to the college in 1956, shortly after the school was made a coeducational institution. The Baptist college's name was changed from Mississippi Woman's College to William Carey College in 1954.

Representatives from Southern Baptist Theological Seminary in Louisville, Ky. and the Winters' alma mater, Westminister Choir College in Princeton, N.J., were among those who brought formal tributes to the couple during a 6 p.m. dinner on Carey's campus.

Dan Hall, director of the Mississippi Baptist Convention's church music department, praised the couple for their "significant contributions to church music" in Mississippi and across the Southern Baptist Convention.

The Carey Chorale, along with several distinguished music alumni, gave a special performance of Handel's Messiah as part of the festivities.

"Rarely does the influence of a husband-wife team almost totally color the growth of any academic program for a quarter of a century," said Carey President Dr. J. Ralph Noonkester.

"Rarer still is the husband-wife team that casts its shadow over an entire discipline, from coast to coast, for a similar span of time. But for the development of church music among Southern Baptists, Donald and Frances Winters constitute such a team."

From the music department's beginning in 1956, Dr. Winters, who retired as dean in 1979, and Mrs. Winters, who retired in 1977 as professor of music, guided the program to national recognition, to school status and established Carey's first graduate-level degree program — the master's in music. Along the way, the school became known for its church and choral music programs.

Before coming to Carey in 1956, Dr. Winters served as acting administrative head of the school of church music at Southern Baptist Theological Seminary. Dr. Winters, along with Mrs. Winters, established the church music program there and was conductor of the seminary's choir, whose annual tours covered more than 100 cities in the South.

He has served as minister of music at Broadway Baptist Church, Louisville, Ky.; First Baptist Church, Bloomington, Ind.; Main Street and First Baptist churches, Hattiesburg; and First Baptist Church, Atlanta.

In 1940, while at First Baptist Church, Atlanta, Dr. and Mrs. Winters established the School of Choirs, which has become known as the graded choir program and is now an institution in churches across the Southern Baptist Convention.

Under Dr. Winters' direction, Carey's chorales appeared at numerous churches, colleges and school assembly programs across the South as well as on several television programs. The groups have performed for the Southern Baptist Convention, the Nationwide Conference on Southern Baptist Musicians and with the Mobile, Ala., Jackson and New Orleans symphony orchestras.

"Donald and Frances Winters have been responsible for giving the school of music its distinct church music program and the naming of the school in their honor reemphasizes Carey's commitment to church and choral music," Noonkester said.

Wednesday, December 5, 1984, Hattiesburg AMERICAN, p. 3A

## DEDICATION

MR. DONALD WINTERS

Because of his outstanding service and contribution to William Carey College, the 1966 CRUSADER is dedicated to Mr. Donald Winters.

Mr. Winters has endeared himself to the students, administration and faculty of Carey. As a teacher he has inspired his students beyond the textbook, as an advisor he has shown great understanding and concern, as a friend he has endeared himself to all who have had the privilege and honor of knowing him.

Professional excellence, personal awareness and strong dedication taste to engender a particular individual.

Mr. Winters from his key console.